**Pursuing Justice and Peace
in South Africa**

Pursuing Justice and Peace in South Africa

Hendrik W. van der Merwe
with a foreword by Adam Curle

ROUTLEDGE
London and New York

First published 1989
by Routledge
11 New Fetter Lane, London EC4P 4EE
29 West 35th Street, New York, NY 10001

© 1989 Hendrik W. van der Merwe
Phototypeset in 10pt Times by
Mews Photosetting, Beckenham, Kent

Printed in Great Britain by
Billing & Sons Ltd, Worcester

All rights reserved. No part of this book may be reprinted or reproduced or utilized in any form or by any electronic, mechanical, or other means, now known or hereafter invented, including photocopying and recording, or in any information storage or retrieval system, without permission in writing from the publishers.

British Library Cataloguing in Publication Data
Van der Merwe, Hendrik Willen
  Pursuing justice and peace in South Africa
  1. South Africa. Apartheid
  I. Title
  323.1'68
ISBN 0-415-03651-8

Library of Congress Cataloging-in-Publication Data
Van der Merwe, Hendrik W.
  Pursuing justice and peace in South Africa.

  Bibliography: p.
  Includes index.
  1. South Africa — Race relations. 2. South Africa — Apartheid. 3. Peace — Religious aspects — Christianity. 4. Justice — Religious aspects — Christianity. I. Title.
  DT63.V36 1989   323.1'196'068   88-36249
ISBN 0-415-03651-8

Contents

Preface		vii
Acknowledgements		ix
Note on Terminology		xi
Foreword by Adam Curle		xiii
1	**Constructive Intervention**	1
	Role tensions between prophets and peacemakers	3
	Injustice, fragmentation, and polarization	4
	Manifest and latent conflict	5
	Empowerment and conciliation	6
2	**Stratification, Inequality, and Conflict**	9
	Dimensions of stratification and conflict	9
	Dimensions of conflict	10
	Apartheid as an ideological force	12
	Towards a synthesis	13
	Conflict and violence	14
	Objective conditions of inequality	17
	Relative deprivation and subjective aspects	19
	Contrasting ideological interpretations of inequality	20
3	**Manifestations of Conflict and Violence**	22
	Race discrimination: 'grand' and 'petty' apartheid	22
	Political repression and militarization	29
	Political protest violence	30
	Township violence	35
	Revolt in education	37
	Consumer protests and boycott	38
	Labour relations	39
	Church–state confrontation	41
	Conclusion	43
4	**Shifting Bases of Conflict, Divisions, and Alliances**	46
	The role of ideology in conflict	46

	The ideology of apartheid	48
	Erosion of the moral base of apartheid	49
	Theological retraction	51
	Reformulation of interests: market vs. controlled economy	53
	Political divisions and alliances in flux	58
5	**Approaches to Handling Conflict**	61
	Pessimistic vs. Utopian schools	62
	Constructive approaches to conflict	62
	Negotiation and coercion	65
	Negotiation, communication, consultation, and co-option	67
	Social and psychological obstacles	68
	Bargaining power, violence, and non-violence	70
	Civil disobedience and conscientious affirmation	74
	Ideological commitment	76
	The siege mentality	76
	The boycott mentality	80
	International sanctions in perspective	81
6	**Third Party Intervention**	87
	The need for intervention	87
	Qualities and tasks of mediators	90
	Neutrality and concern	90
	Improve communication	94
	Identify issues and needs	97
	Helping parties to save face	98
	Private and public roles of mediators	99
	Professional mediation service	103
	Conclusion	104
7	**Prospects for the Constructive Accommodation of Conflict**	105
	Ideological commitment and pragmatic flexibility	105
	Majority rule and white security	108
	Reconciling incremental steps with radical goals	110
	Legitimation and institutionalization of alternative social structures	112
	The pursuit of justice and peace	115
	Bibliography	118
	Index	123

Preface

The pursuit of justice and peace is not an objective academic exercise. It is motivated by a subjective desire to build a better society. In this book I have attempted to spell out my pursuit of these twin goals within the broad academic framework which I have developed as a social scientist.

This is not a source book on South Africa. For background information readers are referred to Graham Leach's *South Africa* published by Routledge and James Leatt *et al.*, *Contending Ideologies in South Africa*, published by David Philip.

I have been motivated partly by the quest for knowledge, but largely by humanitarian concerns. Coming from a conservative rural Afrikaans background, and having actively participated in the Dutch Reformed Church, I have a deep appreciation of the fears of the Afrikaner community. My concern with and sympathy towards the deprived black communities have developed in academic environments over more than three decades. They became more morally and religiously rooted through my involvement in the Religious Society of Friends (Quakers) with whom I have worked closely over the past fifteen years.

Awareness of the grave injustices of the current political system has brought home to me the urgent need for fundamental change to the social structure. The intensification of the struggle, however, has led to increased polarization and the erosion of the middle ground. In recent years I have been responding actively to the great need for mediation and conciliation. This tendency is reflected in this book.

Acknowledgements

This book is the product of the support, cooperation and contributions of a large number of institutions and individuals. I will attempt to list some of these but I take full responsibility for any statements or errors that may appear.

Financial support of various kinds and in diverse forms was given by my employer, the Centre for Intergroup Studies — an autonomous research institute situated on the campus of the University of Cape Town. The Human Sciences Research Council of South Africa made funds available which enabled me to pursue studies abroad in 1986–7. I spent eight months as Friend-in-Residence at Woodbrooke, the international Quaker conference and study centre which is part of the Selly Oak Colleges in Birmingham, England.

Generous grants for travel and research were made available during this period abroad by Quaker Peace and Service (QPS), the service arm of British Quakers (the Religious Society of Friends), the A.B and M.C. Gillett Charitable Trust in England and the Thomas H. and Mary Shoemaker Foundation in the United States of America.

I am indebted to the Quaker Support Group, Adam Curle, Sydney Bailey, Tony Gilpin, John Harding, Bunty Biggs, Trevor Jepson, Alastair Heron, and Muriel Frank — who assisted and supported me under the auspices of Quaker Peace and Service.

Colleagues who have contributed significantly towards ideas in this book include John Hund, Keith Webb, John Groom, John Burton, Ampie Muller, and Johann Maree.

A number of research assistants have made major contributions over many years. These include Sue Williams, who was my assistant at Woodbrooke; Erika Oosthuysen, who compiled most of the material on manifestations of conflict and violence/non-violence; John Hendricks and Odette Geldenhuys, who helped analyze political violence; Yolanda Kleynhans, Selaocwe Setiloane, Wanita Kawa and Kierin O'Malley, who collected material on interest groups; Andries du Toit, who analyzed sources of conflict; and Cathy Philip and André Zaaiman,

Acknowledgements

who contributed significantly to a project on principles of communication.

Administrative staff of the Centre have over the years played an important part in the Centre's programme. They include Helen Albertyn, Petal Ibbotson, Zaida Dinaully, Audrey Allen, Janice Bredeveldt, and Philda Kwetane.

The final presentation of the manuscript was greatly improved by the superior editorial skills of Jean Albert, Gabi Meyer, and Bob Steyn. I am truly grateful to all these people.

Hendrik W. van der Merwe
Director, Centre for Intergroup Studies, Cape Town

Note on Terminology

The following terminology is used when referring to different population groups:

- black instead of the negative 'non-white' as a generic concept
- African instead of 'Bantu' or 'Black'
- coloured people instead of 'Coloureds'
- Indians instead of 'Asians'
- whites instead of 'Whites'

Foreword

by Adam Curle

I feel honoured to write the Foreword of this valuable book by Professor Hendrik W. van der Merwe. It is a rare human being who is sufficiently open minded and wide hearted to offer such an opportunity to one with whom he has engaged in public controversy. Having now, however, a greater understanding of his thought, I see that our differences were largely semantic; our ideas were similar, but we gave them different names — a timely reminder that many human quarrels develop because we use different words for the same things, or the same words for different ones.

The title of this work, *Pursuing Justice and Peace in South Africa*, which of course it does, somewhat belies the fact that what he is talking about is much more universal: how to change society for the better, a problem with which we should all, everywhere, be concerned. This is not a matter of eliminating conflict, but violence. Conflict, as he points out repeatedly and correctly, is not in itself bad.

Here we come up against another of these verbal ambiguities. We tend too easily to equate conflict with the physical violence of war and revolution, maiming and death, but essentially it means a conflict of interest, a difference of opinion. These latter may indeed *lead* to violence, but essentially they constitute the stimulus for change, for examination of stagnant concepts and practices, for healthy argument. Violence, on the other hand, means to harm, basically to do damage to the potential for human development. It means to violate, to rape, another human being and can only be morally justified, if at all, under extraordinary circumstances.

But to oppose violence it is sadly true that we have to sail very close to the wind of ourselves commiting violence. Van der Merwe, as a Quaker (as I am) is not prepared to countenance this. Instead, he proposes — in the second part of the book which is both the most original and the most important — the uses of facilitation (mainly of communications), mediation and negotiation. Significantly, however, he believes that the employment of such methods does not preclude a measure of coercion. In my experience, also, this is sometimes true. Wars may continue while

Foreword

peace negotiations are in progress, each side attempting to add military pressure to the force of diplomacy. Van der Merwe, however, emphatically rejects coercive measures, such as economic boycotts against South Africa that would do violence to the bulk of the African population, especially in the front line states. His account of possible alternative sanctions suggest to me a sort of economic version of the Just War; but I wonder sadly whether such a thing is not, like the Just War, impossible in our ruthless world.

What I find most important, however, is what Hendrik van der Merwe says about his own work. As a South African deeply concerned for the well-being of everyone in his country, as a Quaker who rejects violent solutions, as a social scientist skilled in analyzing social structures, as friend of both white establishment and ANC, as an exceptionally sensitive human being, what he has to say is deeply significant.

He has played, and is playing, a number of different peace-making parts. He tries through his writing, lecturing, personal contacts, and through the work of the Centre he directs, to influence opinion of different parties in the various conflictual relationships with which he is involved — to this extent he is partisan because he propounds a view. He serves as a facilitator trying to get these parties into constructive touch with each other, whether opposing African groups or ANC with White leaders — here he is completely impartial. He mediates between different groups, trying to find and propound ways of resolving the differences that separate them; here he is helped by his rational social analysis. As a negotiator, although he says relatively little about this particular role, he sometimes plays a part in the bargaining or horse-trading which is the basis of that process. He concludes that the most important aspects of third party intervention are facilitation probably leading on to mediation which, in a case of extreme polarization as in South Africa, are to be seen not as a substitute for but as complementary to coercion on the establishment.

Hendrik is undoubtedly in a hideously difficult position. To the extent that in one role he must remain impartial, he is likely to be unpopular with everyone! To the extent that, as a facilitator, he is in contact with, for example, the ANC, he is easily seen as hostile to the government or to powerful elements such as the police that can make his life difficult.

The work of mediators or go-betweens is always difficult in any case. The protagonists with whom they deal try to make use of them for their own ends. They also mistrust them; for how could they really be their friends, if as they claim, they are also the friends of their enemies? And how do they know that they are not *agents provocateurs* of some sort? But the position of someone working in his or her own country is immeasurably more complex. They are *part of the situation they are attempting to alter*. How can they balance the necessary impartiality with the equally necessary partisanship of change? How can someone like

Hendrik van der Merwe avoid the inner tensions and contradictions of what the psychoanalysts call 'doubled (and in his case, sometimes treble, I suspect) role trouble'? It is a great tribute to his courage and determination that he persists in this psychologically — if not perhaps at times physically — dangerous work. It is a balancing act that only someone of great skill and dedication could sustain.

I would now also partly attribute the mild disagreements we have had in the past to the contrast between the necessary overlapping of roles in his setting with my definitions based on operating in a scene far from home where I was not faced with these contradictions.

We must, however, learn how to operate in our home environment. It is to be hoped that in a normal (if such a thing exists) democratic system, the political structure will enable us to work for social changes that reduce violence and promote joint problem solving by contending groups. But in too many places this is not possible. New skills are needed which relate mediatory abilities and partisan persuasion to active non-violence of the Gandhian type (a powerful form of coercion) and negotiation.

I am not sure if this is what Hendrik has in mind in proposing a professional mediation service, but I suspect that the development of and the training for acquiring such skills would present a formidable challenge to many of our social science — and indeed, social — conventions. Nor am I sure that the proponents of these skills would be readily accepted — in some places they would certainly be hounded, however peaceful and altruistic, as revolutionaries. But we live in desperate times and desperate times demand comparable remedies if our faltering civilization is to be transformed.

Chapter one

Constructive Intervention

Justice is achieved not by enforcing law and order, but by creating a just society whose members are assured of the opportunity to realise their human potential. A society may be termed just 'when its members live together with the confident expectation that their relations and transactions, their customs and law will be fair and beneficial to all' (Southern African Catholic Bishops' Conference, 1985: 99). A just society presupposes enjoyment by all members of basic human rights. Human rights are open to debate. For purposes of this discussion, however, human rights will be assumed to include equality and protection under the law, rights to family life, freedom of movement and of association and choice of residence, a share in economic resources to meet basic needs, and a full share in decisions affecting the life of the individual and the community.

Similarly, peace is more than the absence of war or overt physical conflict. Thus the task of peacemaking must not be seen as smoothing over deep divisions in society and leaving the causes of division unaddressed. Peace has negative and positive aspects. The negative aspect is absence of something — absence of turmoil, tension, violence, and war. The positive side of peace is 'a condition of good management, orderly resolution of conflict, harmony associated with mature relationships, gentleness and love' (Boulding 1978: 3). A distinction should therefore be drawn between *apparent* peace, where there is 'law and order' without real justice, and *stable* peace, where there is fairness and justice.

Justice and peace cannot be equated with the maintenance of the *status quo* in South Africa. Therefore the pursuit of justice and peace implies fundamental social change.

There is a complementary and contrasting relationship between justice and peace as desirable goals in South Africa and between the problems which inhibit their attainment and the means by which they are pursued. This intertwined relationship is illustrated in Figure 1.

Three observations must be made about the goals of justice and peace.

Figure 1 The constructive intervention model for the accommodation of conflict

THE PROBLEMS	INEQUALITY INJUSTICE VIOLENCE	(RACE) DISCRIMINATION FRAGMENTATION POLARIZATION VIOLENCE
	Economic, material Political Socio-cultural	Racial and ethnic Economic, material Political Ideological
THE MEANS	EMPOWERMENT DEVELOPMENT COERCION	RECONCILIATION
	Education Coercion Violence and non-violence Political empowerment Community development	Negotiation Mediation Facilitation Removal of race discrimination Peacemaking Non-violence
THE GOALS	SOCIAL JUSTICE EQUALITY HUMAN RIGHTS	PEACE CONCILIATION

The first is that they are *ideals* for society and are in fact unattainable. We can never have full justice or peace in society. We can only strive towards them. To pretend that we could at any stage achieve a situation of complete justice or peace in South Africa, or in any other country, would be highly misleading. To claim, as the authorities sometimes do, that we have a peaceful society, is equally misleading. Apartheid society, quite apart from the violence of political protest, is a violent society.

The second point about these two goals is that they are complementary — we cannot have one without the other. There can be no justice without peace nor can there be peace without justice. Peacemaking must therefore be concerned with promoting justice. Gross inequality amounts to injustice. Therefore promotion of justice and peace in South Africa must involve removal of fundamental disparities in social, economic, and political matters. At the same time, without reconciliation or the accommodation of differences, a society tears itself apart and neither peace nor justice can exist.

The third observation is that these goals stand in a relation of tension to each other. Sometimes justice appears to be unattainable by peaceful means, and at times the achievement of peace seems to run counter to the demand for justice. This tension becomes more obvious in the interaction and contrast between two different means for pursuing these two goals (i.e. between the roles of prophets and peacemakers).

Role tensions between prophets and peacemakers

The peacemaker or conciliator must have credibility on all sides of a conflict. Building and maintaining good relations and credibility with all parties is not compatible with attacks on injustice or public confrontation with the perceived perpetrators of injustice. The roles, tasks, and styles of peacemakers and prophets are different. And this difference can cause severe tension within any one person or group, and among persons and groups.

The peacemaker, who is trying to make peace at all costs, is likely to underplay injustice and overlook its manifestations. By doing so he may be able to arrange some kind of truce or apparent peace, but this will leave patterns and relations of inequality and injustice unchanged. The weaker or deprived party will want an assurance that the intervener will not be obsessed with peacemaking only, but will also be concerned with promoting justice.

To what extent can the intermediary express himself on issues of injustice without confronting or offending one party? It *is* possible to express concern about a problem, an injustice, an atrocity, without attributing blame. But to do so in practice is a fine art. Neither genuine concern nor non-judgmentalism can be taught in academic courses on peacemaking.

In conflict situations where injustice is not a primary issue, or where mediators can be seen as completely detached, these problems are less severe. In South Africa, however, injustice is seen as *the* primary issue by the deprived groups and by the international community. Furthermore, apartheid has become an international issue and no citizen of any other country is seen as detached or neutral.

Justice in South Africa has become an obsession in the anti-apartheid movement leading to the slogan: 'There can be no peace until there is justice.'

This atmosphere contributes to the discrediting of moves towards conciliation or peacemaking. Given the complementary relationship of the twin goals of peace and justice, and that justice is an ideal state that can never be fully achieved, the slogan that peacemaking should be shelved, or even opposed, until justice has been achieved, obviously implies that peacemaking is not really on the agenda.

Just as peace and justice as goals are complementary to one another, peacemaking and promotion of justice as *means* towards these goals are also complementary; one should not be promoted without the other. Obsession with promotion of immediate, total justice at all costs will undermine progress towards peace and, therefore, any hope of a stable, lasting society. What kind of justice can there be without peace?

The styles and roles of prophets and peacemakers are very different. As individuals differ in personality, and organizations differ in goals and functions, each individual and organization will obviously lean more towards one role than the other. These tensions are reflected in this book, especially through illustrations that I give from my own experiences. I tend to respond to the particular needs of the groups I am dealing with, and to specific situations.

During the 1976 revolt I set off as a neutral intervener between government officials and black community leaders but I spontaneously shifted towards a more partisan stand in support of the deprived groups. I attributed this shift to two factors: my response to the needs of the black community at that time, and the fact that one cannot be neutral on moral issues (Van der Merwe 1983a).

During the immense security clampdown in the early 1980s I was a member of a delegation of the South African Institute of Race Relations to a regional head of police. The delegation's intention was to bring reported atrocities and police torture to his notice in a friendly way. But the meeting developed into a confrontation. With the permission of my colleagues, I withdrew from the delegation while the meeting was in progress because I believed my role as a go-between would be more constructive and valuable than merely adding my voice to the protest movement. Subsequent developments gave support to that step when local police co-operated with a team of civilian peace marshals to control a crowd at a meeting addressed by Bishop Desmond Tutu under the auspices of the Institute of Race Relations (Van der Merwe 1986b).

In recent years I have tended to respond increasingly to the need for conciliation in South Africa, but the art of peacemaking requires constant vigilance to maintain a balanced and sensitive approach. There are no scientific recipes or easy answers.

In the light of the goals we would like to achieve in South Africa, the current situation could be described in terms of two major problems: injustice and polarization.

Injustice, fragmentation, and polarization

In any society there is a degree of inequality which may be regarded as normal. But in South Africa there is gross inequality which amounts to injustice.

For analytical purposes, I distinguish between three major dimensions of inequality: economic, political, and socio-cultural. These dimensions refer to distinctions to be made in Chapter 2, where I analyze conflict in more detail and where I argue that the nature of conflict in South Africa is multi-dimensional and that the relative importance of dimensions should be determined by empirical analysis.

Fundamentally, my argument is that any attempts to move towards greater equality and greater justice should be embodied in a multi-dimensional programme.

The second problem — polarization — concerns the breakdown of communication and relationships among different groups. While race constitutes the single most important factor in determining inequality in South Africa and therefore also the greatest measure of injustice, race discrimination constitutes *only one and no longer the major component of polarization or estrangement between groups in South Africa*.

I have used the word polarization to describe tension between groups. But we should more accurately speak of fragmentation of relationships in South Africa, as there are no two clearly polarized groups. There is a whole range of conflicting elements, and these conflicts are ideological, religious, economic, and so on. There are no two single groups opposing each other. Groups are polarized in the sense that people are driven out of the centre into sharply-defined groups. Often ideological conflict rather than economic inequality constitutes a major source of division.

Although analytical distinctions are made between injustice based on racial inequality and polarization based partly on race discrimination, there is a dynamic interplay between these two problems. One influences the other. I will indicate later how difficult it often is to distinguish in real life and, especially, in scientific measurement between the relative importance of race and class in determining relationships in South Africa, or for that matter in any other society.

Like the goals of justice and peace, the problems of injustice and polarization are in some ways complementary. Discrimination and injustice tend to alienate people, drive them apart, and sharpen the distinctions between them. And polarization tends to promote injustice by focusing attention on differences between separated groups. This makes it easier for each to see the other as less than human, so that awareness of injustice fails to transcend group boundaries.

Manifest and latent conflict

In Chapter 4 I make a distinction between manifest and latent (or potential) conflict. This distinction is important for identifying emerging divisions within society at an early stage. The analyst, planner, and politician can thus anticipate emerging problems and plan accordingly. One of my arguments is that the fundamental shift in the nature of conflict in South Africa raises a distinct danger. We may fail to identify the changing fundamental issues at an early stage and, therefore, fail to direct our attention and efforts to the most crucial problems.

Empowerment and conciliation

Having identified the major problems and also the goals that we want to pursue, we turn then to the means or methods that can be employed to achieve these goals. The two major means I identify are: development and empowerment to achieve greater justice, and mediation and conciliation as means towards peace.

Development includes a whole range of activities and programmes concerned with deprived groups. I would single out the political component of empowerment, on the assumption that in most political situations, and particularly in South Africa, power is the key component in the political process. The nature of the problem in our situation of racial inequality and of injustice clearly indicates the need for greater symmetry of power; that is, the need for realistic bargaining power for politically weaker communities. Development, however, incorporates a much wider range of activities than political empowerment, including for example education, training, confidence-building, community organization, and development of leadership.

I will argue that empowerment is an essential element in enabling deprived groups in South Africa to achieve their own liberation and their own system of justice. This contrasts with power intervention by outside bodies attempting to impose some kind of settlement on South Africa. It is highly desirable that symmetry or balance be achieved by internal groups rather than through outside elements or superpowers. An internal settlement would be far more stable than any kind of settlement imposed by external superpowers, which would merely ensure outside control and leave the internal situation inherently unstable.

Attempts to create peace out of conflict are referred to in terms such as settlement, resolution, management, or accommodation of conflict.

Settlement has the connotation of determination by a third party, such as a court or a greater power. This could be a compromise which parties feel they have to accept, but which they have no personal interest in upholding. Resolution, on the other hand, implies a final solution freely acceptable to all parties — one that does not destroy important values and that the parties will not wish to repudiate under ordinary circumstances.

In United Nations' terminology, 'peaceful' or 'pacific' settlement of disputes refers to settlement without violence, but not necessarily without coercion. This often means that the violence of parties is merely suppressed by coercion. Such settlements cannot assure political stability, since shifts in power relations or removal of an outside force are likely to lead to the re-emergence of the conflict.

I will refer later to mediation and conciliation efforts aimed at enabling the conflicting parties to negotiate together in efforts to accommodate the conflict as constructively as possible. I use the term 'conflict accommodation' as a generic term to include all methods, practices, and techniques — formal and informal, traditional and alternative, within and outside the courts — that are used to resolve or settle disputes.

The term 'conciliation' suggests finding ways of living together in some kind of agreed pragmatic relationship which will not necessarily be ideal. In reality, political adversaries are very often interacting in a state of tension and even hatred. The fundamental argument in this process of conciliation is that the parties should find ways of living together as partners even though they may not be in an easy relationship with one another. The concept of conciliation in South Africa implies in the first place the normalization of race relations. As I have already indicated, it also implies conciliation among a whole range of conflicting interest groups.

In relatively peaceful situations parties would be able to enter into negotiations with one another to establish stable relationships in some form of agreed framework or political system. Where two parties are in fundamental disagreement, at war, unable or unwilling to communicate directly with each other, however, a third party or intermediary must intervene to establish communication between the parties, so that necessary changes can be explored. I will discuss in detail the need for intervention and will consider various aspects of mediation.

This process of conciliation or mediation goes beyond improvement of communication between parties within an existing framework. I argue that, in South Africa, communication is not enough. There is also a need for structural reform in the society. The social structure requires fundamental change. This applies both to the political system, which requires a new constitution, and to the socio-economic system, which now allows for excessive exploitation by large economic concerns and preserves disproportionate social power and prestige in the hands of relatively few people. The present economic system would certainly require political intervention to ensure a fairer distribution of the wealth and resources of the country.

This understanding of conciliation highlights the interplay between the goals of justice and peace, and between the problems of injustice and polarization. The further implication of this interplay is that the chief means for achieving these two goals — empowerment and negotiation — are also complementary. There is a direct and necessary interplay between these two which I shall pursue later.

Some methods, means and forms of action discussed in relation to empowerment include various kinds of pressures, seen as essential for bringing about change in South Africa. I argue that there will be no fundamental change in the country without considerable pressure on the establishment. We must take for granted that the whites, and now also the wider group who have achieved privileged positions, will not willingly sacrifice these positions. For people to protect their vested interests is normal in any society. The moral force within the establishment is not strong enough to bring about change willingly. I argue for constructive rather than punitive pressures. These are more likely to succeed in promoting a form of justice not merely imposed on the society, but achieved through both negotiation and coercion.

Chapter two

Stratification, Inequality, and Conflict

Dimensions of stratification and conflict

Political action requires clear policies, programmes, slogans. This requirement tempts political leaders or politically-conscious academics to interpret complex situations in simple terms. Where there is multi-dimensional conflict, one single dimension may be singled out.

Aside from these practical motivations there is also strong ideological motivation to oversimplify complex situations. Rigid deterministic interpretations of stratification patterns and the nature of conflict in South Africa are propagated by various schools of thought.

In this chapter I discuss the nature of stratification in South Africa, the extent to which it underlies conflict, and the major dimensions of that conflict.

I define *social stratification* as the differentiation of society into hierarchically superimposed units in accordance with invidious standards. These standards may represent the common value system of the community or they may be objectively imposed by those in power. This definition suggests not only that there are two types or bases of stratification, but also that there are two basically different approaches to the study of stratification.

The first approach emphasizes the functional nature of stratification. It is reflected in the writings of conservative historians and sociologists, and in the politics of conservative apartheid politicians in South Africa. On the other hand, social scientists in the 'dialectic' or 'conflict' tradition tend to emphasize the imposed nature of stratification and the animosity between two polarized, opposed groups with conflicting interests. These views are represented in radical political circles in South Africa.

Both these conflicting approaches are realities for the parties or classes involved. The first approach represents the highly subjective view of those in favour of the *status quo*. Nevertheless, it is a true and real reflection of their view of the world in which they live. The conflict approach, on the other hand, reflects the subjective response to the bitter reality experienced by the underdog.

Apart from these subjective realities there is an objective reality: the actual distribution of economic security and privilege, political power, and social status or prestige among the population. Analysis of stratification in South Africa should present both the objective factual situation and the full range of subjective perspectives.

Dimensions of conflict

Interpretation of stratification and inequality as sources of conflict will be related to one's views on the nature and causes of conflict. The debate about causes of conflict in South Africa and about the nature of apartheid has been consistently oversimplified in relation to race, ethnicity, class, nationalism, language, and religion.

Conflict in plural societies can be examined within three major dimensions of stratification: the economic, the political, and the socio-cultural. These are of course closely related but the precise nature of the interrelationship is a matter of some dispute.

The importance of each dimension varies from one situation to the next, being closely related to immediate social conditions and prevailing cultural values. In more advanced industrial nations, key resources of property, occupation, education, and membership in the most powerful political class tend to be held by the same persons. So it is often difficult, if not impossible, to disentangle one form of class struggle from another (Hanf *et al.* 1981: 10). Conflicts between racial, ethnic, and religious status groups become entangled with the conflict between economic classes.

Lenski (1966: 423-4) argues that it is often difficult to determine to what extent the struggles of deprived blacks are economic class struggles and to what extent they are status-group struggles.

Various hierarchies of stratification are thus interrelated but not identical; their interrelationships must be carefully examined because not all communities attach equal importance to the various dimensions of stratification. For example, some communities may value education more highly than material possessions and vice versa.

If we are interested in the subjective experience of the members of a community we need to understand their underlying values and expectations. Social stratification is a system of interpersonal relationships that is socially recognized and conforms with prevailing norms and rules of conduct. Because these behaviour patterns are carried over from generation to generation they undergo change over time. Social stratification is always connected with other aspects of society. There are institutional links with politics, kinship, marriage and the family, economics, education, and religion. Racial stratification and political and economic power are clearly very closely associated in South Africa, as those who control capital decide on the patterns of production, services, wage levels, and working conditions.

The relative importance and interrelationships of the dimensions of conflict in a given society should be treated as empirical rather than purely theoretical questions.

To understand and assess the nature and severity of conflict one has to investigate and analyze basic values and perceptions. There is no simple explanation or cause of major conflicts:

> However we may yearn for simple explanations, there is no reason to assume that a whole complex of human woes can be attributed to one prime cause or even to a limited number of causes. It is far more likely that each major catastrophe is rooted in multiple specific causes and conditions, and that it must be explained through a particular 'mix' of interrelationships.
>
> (Glaser and Possony 1979: 5)

While large-scale economic inequality in South Africa constitutes potential for serious conflict, actual conflict will depend on how it is perceived by the participants, especially the deprived. As Hanf *et al.* (1981: 27) write: 'Do they regard economic inequality as the outcome of their historically determined unequal origins, or of conscious manipulation on the part of the dominant group? Is it perceived as "class conflict", "racial conflict", or as a combination of both?'

Needs and aspirations are not absolute. They change over time and vary in different groups as rising expectations generate new standards. The identification of basic needs is an important task of the conflict analyst.

One school of thought emphasizes the economic dimension, believing that conflict is caused by cleavages between classes which have opposing economic interests. This school holds that conflicts in plural societies are in the final analysis class struggles, even when they manifest as ethnic, racial, linguistic, or religious conflicts.

Under the influence of Marx, conflict theorists have taken class conflict as *normal* and have regarded allegiance to ethnic and national groupings as problematic, to be explained in terms of false consciousness (Rex 1981: 87).

The neo-Marxist interpretation of South Africa's capitalist development holds that the fundamental class cleavages in South Africa are the result of capitalist modes of production. Thus Cosmas Desmond (1978: 88–90) argues that the basic objective of the Nationalists is 'the control of political power as the means of protecting their economic interests'.

The capitalist ruling class is prepared to employ any means to keep the costs of the labour factor of production as low as possible and profits as high as possible, and it will use political and administrative manipulation and discrimination to achieve its goal. Racial discrimination is therefore seen as a function of capitalism.

The political dimension is crucial. Groups and group cleavages, be they economic or cultural, do not exist in a vacuum; they are politically manipulated — Schermerhorn (1970) emphasizes the importance of domination and coercion in political systems in plural societies.

Some writers attach great importance to the socio-cultural dimensions of conflict, believing that an individual's primary loyalty is not to class but to a basic social group within a plural society: ethnic, racial, linguistic, or religious. In fact serious conflicts often arise between people who belong to similar social classes but to different cultural groups. Greenberg (1980: 14, 15) points out that social and historical contexts rather than race often explain the development of group identities in the United States and southern Africa.

In conflict situations, interplay between class, status, and power criteria is always complex. Revolutions and group conflicts are frequently based on race, ethnicity, and religion, rather than on the class struggle.

Apartheid as an ideological force

Verwoerd developed the idea of apartheid into an ideology.

> Until 1948, segregation and discrimination were used pragmatically as instruments of white minority rule. Separation was applied if it was 'practical', i.e. where it served the interests of the minority and when it was convenient. However, when clothed in the concept of apartheid, racial segregation became an official ideology. Principles prevailed over pragmatic considerations or public interest; they were applied without regard for the immediate benefits, rather than opportunistically. The ruling minority was expected to stand by these principles, regardless of the sacrifices this might demand.
> (Hanf *et al* 1981: 34)

Accepting that ideology is a pattern of ideas both functional and evaluative, which purports to explain and legitimize the social structure and culture of a particular social group, it becomes clear that classic apartheid can only be discarded if the socio-political system in which it is rooted is radically reconstructed.

There is an important and close connection between nationhood and the specifically South African interpretation of Calvinist teachings. Afrikanerdom is deeply identified with the Dutch Reformed Churches, which traditionally took an official stand on the apartheid ideology. It was believed that it was the Will of God that races and people live separately, each with its own language and culture. In the light of this, racial segregation in the church was not only permitted but a Christian duty. Racial segregation was unequivocally justified. The crucial point here is that the Afrikaner is simultaneously aware of himself as an Afrikaner and as a member of a religious group. This imparts an extraordinary emotional depth to his concept of ethnic nationhood (Hanf *et al* 1981: 36).

The theological and ideological bases of apartheid have been emphasized frequently. Responding to the current trend to explain apartheid according to purely or largely economic or neo-Marxist principles, Charles Villa-Vicencio writes (1977: 373):

> To regard apartheid as a pragmatic policy designed merely to preserve the privileges and to institutionalise the avarice of White South Africans is to grossly underestimate the ardent and religious commitment of White nationalists.

He concludes that 'The political problem of South Africa is a theological one.' The theological doctrine of the Afrikaner, plus his 'irrational obsession that it is his unique divine calling to preserve the existence of the White race, is the basis of White intransigence in South Africa today' (1977: 382). The gradual crumbling of this theological base is discussed in Chapters 4 and 7.

Towards a synthesis

There appears to be general acceptance of the three dimensional model of stratification. There is also evidence that class, power, and status can be independent of one another.

> If there is any general conclusion to be drawn . . . , it is surely that inequalities of all three kinds can under at least some circumstances arise autonomously, and that the causal relations between the three are sometimes in one direction and sometimes in another. Thus the relation between wealth and power may be directly reversed depending on the stage of economic or political development reached by the society in question.
>
> (Runciman 1968: 40–1)

Hanf *et al.* (1981: 12) summarize their conclusion as follows:

> There are many plural societies, and the severity of conflict within

them varies widely . . . For example, differences between economic interests in plural societies may or may not develop into conflicts within cultural groups, or between them. Moreover, cultural group conflict can arise irrespective of the economic situation. Finally, economic and cultural conflicts may or may not determine the pattern of political conflict in plural societies. In sum, the economic, cultural, and political dimensions of conflict may coincide in some plural societies, and run counter to one another in others. It is quite possible that, in a given plural society, one group is economically dominant, another culturally and a third politically. Furthermore, cleavages may cross-cut in some dimensions and coincide in others. So it is surely implausible to stipulate in principle that one dimension of conflict will be primary. And the context of conflict itself may change: the cause of conflict in some previous situation may be different from that in the current context.

In spite of the pronouncements of zealous ideologists, shifts in ideologies do take place.

A major defect of the Marxist view of class consciousness and class interests is that it takes a monistic economic view of the forces that move men to behave as they do. Behaviour in society is always the product of several interrelated social interests. Many social factors influence attitudes towards economic and social interests. Some of these factors that cut across broad class positions are ethnic origin, regional factors, size of community, religion, and race. Class can never be understood apart from culture, ethnicity, race, and nationality.

Conflict and violence

Although most of us have been conditioned into regarding conflict as an unpleasant word, conflict is neutral, not negative. Outwardly it is simply the manifestation of the fact that people think and behave differently, according to their individual social and personal histories. It also occurs as a response to frustration and some would say as an expression of aggressive and competitive instincts. Inner conflict reflects our difficulties in coming to terms with life's challenges.

The most valuable aspect of conflict is the energy it generates. Conflict management is not an attempt to suppress this energy, but to channel it constructively.

Conflict caused by differing viewpoints may lead to harsh and painful situations or it can be transformed into creative and productive dialogue. Conflict will become easier to manage if we see it as inevitable but not necessarily destructive, and as a problem to be solved rather than a battle to be won.

(Albert 1986: 4)

Conflict can be defined in terms of both structural (material) and ideological issues. Structural conflict flows out of contradictory claims to scarce resources, economic privilege, political power, and social status. As discussed in the previous section, these three dimensions can be measured objectively; yet their *relative importance* within the personal and societal value system is a matter of great debate. This confirms the contention that any analysis of conflict must distinguish clearly between objective and subjective bases of conflict.

Different types of conflict can be viewed as manifestations of friction between different 'interest groups'. We are concerned, in particular, with conflict between disadvantaged groups and powerful or entrenched groups from whom advantage must be won.

Objective and *subjective* bases of conflict must be clearly separated. Failure to do so results in excessively psycho-logistic explanations which cannot do justice to the structure of conflict in society. Social conflict and hostile sentiment are separate phenomena. It is not necessarily true that objective discrepancies in class (wealth), status, and power will result in conflict between groups.

The way individuals define their situation, as well as the objective features of the situation, must be analyzed. Intergroup justice, like intergroup conflict, is based on perceptions of what exists and of what is legitimate. Thus group conflict must be studied in terms of social definitions.

The impact of conflict varies according to the type of social structure. In open democratic societies, conflict that aims at the resolution of tension is likely to have stabilizing functions. Multiple affiliations of individuals cause them to participate in a variety of group conflicts and those who are antagonists in one conflict may be allies in another. Thus cleavage along one axis is prevented. The more integrated into the society the conflicting parties are, the less likely it is that the conflict between them will be violent. Thus research on conflict can highlight the importance of democracy in the process of peaceful change and can point the way to a more open society.

Ideological conflict refers to a conflict of values, beliefs and perceptions. Goals and values can acquire ideological meaning and may motivate people to act independently of their objective structural position.

The sources of conflict are directly relevant to the process of accommodation. Since structural resources are usually finite and material, contradictory claims may be difficult or impossible to reconcile. To the extent that these resources are rationally developed and exploited, however, the contending parties may find a *modus vivendi* based on a non-emotional cost analysis aimed at maximum gain for each.

Values and ideologies, on the other hand, are essentially subjective, and do not concern finite resources directly. Conflicts of values should therefore be more amenable to resolution by the mere adaptation and adjustment of opinions and attitudes. This is, however, not the case — the ideologizing of conflict usually leads to its intensification. Ideological commitment leads to intolerance, polarization, and a refusal to compromise. This highlights the role of ideologists in conflict. Ideologists tend to strip conflicts of their merely personal or group aspect, and transform them into struggles over eternal verities. They thereby deepen and intensify them.

Conflict and consensus are correlative. Both are part of the dialectic of social life. It thus seems inadvisable to distinguish too sharply between a consensus model and a conflict model of society. Conflict is a natural endemic condition of society and can serve positive functions, provided it is channelled and accommodated constructively.

Violence, the use of force to injure, harm, or constrain someone, is an extreme manifestation of destructive conflict. It is a result of the failure to accommodate conflict successfully, or to regulate it. Violence refers to behaviour or sanctions which violate the dignity and integrity of an individual or a group. We define it as the application of force, action, motive or thought in such a way (overt, covert, direct or indirect) that a person or group is injured, controlled or destroyed in a physical, psychological or spiritual sense.

Traditionally, the word violence used to be associated only with physical acts used by people in protest. In recent years the concepts of structural or institutional violence were formulated. Violence committed through the legal machinery and institutions of the social system or the state is referred to as institutional or structural violence, which is the restriction of choices available to some part of a community through either laws or customs which create inequalities of opportunity or treatment (Teichman 1986: 26-7).

The actions of the state are usually described as 'force' which is sanctioned by law. Violence is improper use of force. The concept of institutional violence is therefore unacceptable to conservative thinkers and supporters of the status quo. President Kaunda of Zambia points out how history is written by the victor and how 'violence has always been defined by the powerful rather than the weak, the oppressor rather than the oppressed' (1980: 127). In spite of being in a ruling position himself he states bluntly:

> I refuse to cloud the issue by such word-play. Anything which hurts a human being is violence, and there is no point in beating about the bush. With some exceptions, the power which establishes a state is

violence; the power which maintains it is violence; the power which eventually overthrows it is violence...

(Kaunda 1980: 41)

While violence is usually abhorred in public rhetoric, it is almost as endemic as conflict. This is due to many factors, including the generally accepted view that violence *does* work, the relative aggressiveness of human nature, and the fact that (with the exception of a minute percentage of universal pacifists), war is accepted by all mankind as a legitimate instrument of last resort. All nations recognize the validity of violence in pursuit or protection of national interests.

In South Africa the selective use of the terms 'violence' and 'force' reflect political biases. Conservatives describe government action as force and opposition action as violence, while radicals do the opposite.

In the *Kairos Document*, and in a subsequent publication, *Theology and Violence*, the South African government is seen as illegitimate and the use of the words force and violence is reversed. To quote only one example: '. . . if it is legitimate to use violence to support such a regime it is also legitimate to use force to destroy it. . . ' (Villa-Vicencio 1987: 7).

Objective conditions of inequality

Attitudes, beliefs and values as well as structural conditions produce political violence. We need to look at both the objective, structural conditions of inequality and the subjective aspects such as relative deprivation, to understand conflict and violence in South Africa.

Empirical data overwhelmingly support the assertion that there is a clear causal link between social conflict and structural social inequality. Economic inequality can occur through a gradation of income from high to low, but in many societies there are excessive concentrations of wealth in the upper strata and of poverty in the lower strata, reflecting a disturbingly clear dichotomy between rich and poor.

The direct relationship between race and class is quite clear in many areas: ownership of land and means of production, average income, occupational status, per capita expenditure on education, life expectancy, physical and mental health, to name the most important.

According to the 1985 census, the total population of the Republic of South Africa was about 23.4 million. Whites accounted for slightly less than 20 per cent of this total and Africans for almost 65 per cent. These figures, however, are misleading. It was estimated that Africans were undercounted by over four million. Furthermore, the independent homelands (the so-called TBVC countries — Transkei, Bophuthatswana, Venda, and Ciskei) form such an integral part of the Republic that their populations should be included.

The total population for South Africa and the TBVC countries estimated by the Development Bank of Southern Africa amounts to 33.67 million of which whites accounted for only 14.7 per cent and Africans, numbering 25 million, accounted for 74.3 per cent (Eberstadt 1988: 22).

Ownership and control of land is a fundamental source of economic and political power in any country. While Africans predominate in numbers in all parts of South Africa they are deprived of property rights in 86.3 per cent of the country. They are also effectively prevented from owning and controlling the means of production in the country. Going by the most objective data, Hanf *et al.* (1981: 27) argue

> that there is large-scale economic inequality in South Africa. A minority has a virtual monopoly on the ownership of the means of production, receives the largest share of the national income, and enjoys a much higher standard of living. The majority is at a disadvantage. . . Thus, class conflict and racial conflict coincide.

Racial inequality is especially conspicuous in the comparison of income of the racial groups. In 1983 the estimated per capita real disposable income for whites was R6,242, for Africans in the metropolitan areas R1,366 and for Africans in the non-growth areas R388 (Eberstadt 1988: 23). In 1984 the average monthly earnings of a white was R1,403 and that of an African R363 (SAIRR 1985: 368).

Inequality in educational opportunities is reflected in the low per capita state expenditure on black education. Estimated public expenditure per white school pupil in 1984 was R1,926 and per African pupil R293 (SAIRR 1985: 368).

The gross economic inequalities in South Africa have direct impact on life-chances, as can be seen from the fact that the average life expectancy at birth of a white male in 1980 was 66.6 years, while that of a coloured male was 54.3 years (Eberstadt 1988: 24).

Malnutrition is no longer a notifiable disease in South Africa, and thus no official statistics are available, but reports indicate widespread malnutrition among African children. The African infant mortality rate is estimated to be between 9 and 10 times higher than that of whites. The official infant mortality rate for whites in 1985 was 9.7 deaths per thousand live births, for Asians 15.6, and for coloured people 40.4 (Eberstadt 1988: 26).

The objective conditions of inequality make it clear that South Africa is a highly stratified society, characterized by intense structural and institutional injustice and violence.

Relative deprivation and subjective aspects

Some forms of economic deprivation can be defined in absolute terms relating to biological needs for food, shelter, and clothing. When people have insufficient income to meet these needs they are suffering from *actual* measurable or assessable deprivation. Political and social deprivation, however, are not easily defined except in *comparative* terms. Individuals and groups are deprived in political or social terms insofar as they have less political power or social benefits than others, but this deprivation only attains meaning when a comparison is actually drawn.

People's attitudes, aspirations, and grievances depend largely on their consciousness of their situation, particularly in contrast with others more or less fortunate. The intensity with which deprivation is felt may be out of all proportion to the actual amount of deprivation. People who are relatively deprived, in the sense of having fewer luxuries than others, may be more discontented than those who are deprived of the minimum physical needs. Objective structural inequalities provide the potential for conflict but subjective perceptions of these differences determine whether or not these inequalities will lead to conflict.

Extreme poverty, when combined with ignorance, breeds that lack of desire for better things which has been called 'wantlessness' — the resigned acceptance of a subhuman lot. But extreme poverty, when it is combined with the knowledge that some societies are affluent, breeds envious desires and the expectation that these desires must of necessity, and very soon, be satisfied.

Slaves who submissively accept their subordinate position as natural will not easily organize a revolt against their oppressors. On the other hand, a subordinate group in which the members believe that their subordinate position is the result of unjust and arbitrarily enforced discrimination and suppression, will be virtually programmed for conflict (Rhoodie 1983: 86).

Grievances are not always consciously formulated or articulated. Often people are not aware that they have common grievances around which they could justifiably organise themselves to bring their complaints to the attention of the authorities. The lack of formal channels of access to authority contributes towards this lack of expression. African women, for example, are among the most disadvantaged in South African society, but their specific grievances tend to remain unarticulated. They are often, by the nature of their employment (e.g. domestic work), isolated from others with the same problems and thus are unlikely to become aware of and organize around their common grievances. Conflict in this sphere tends to remain latent. To sum up, social conflict revolves around the collective perceptions of social inequality and injustice and is spurred on by organization around these issues.

Contrasting ideological interpretations of inequality

Gross racial inequality and stratification are major sources of conflict in South Africa. However, apart from the conflict between rich and poor, there is also a fundamental division between two perspectives on inequality and stratification — the conservative functionalist view and the radical conflict view.

Social inequality is ubiquitous and universal and many people regard it as functional because it performs valuable and important functions in society. Writers holding these views are sometimes referred to as functionalists, conservatives, or traditionalists. They argue that it is by means of the stratification system that hostility among diverse elements is kept to a minimum and solidarity and integration are achieved. In their view it is a traditional and tested way of distributing unlike and unequal functions among unlike and unequal people and groups. It provides a natural division of labour and distribution of authority — an indispensable ingredient in the maintenance of orderly society.

This conservative approach to stratification, which emphasizes its spontaneous and voluntary nature, is reflected in the views of 'consensus historians', sociologists in the 'functionalist' tradition, and the supporters of apartheid. Social scientists in the 'dialectic' or 'conflict' tradition emphasize the fact that inequality is enforced by privileged groups at the expense of the masses and they stress the element of animosity between two polarized, opposed groups with conflicting interests.

The conservative and radical views of South African society are ideal types, and no single group — political or academic — fits perfectly into either.

Conservative politicians, writers, and academics emphasize the positive functions of the stratification system in South Africa, and the historial 'benevolence' of the whites towards the indigenous population. They recall that indigenous populations were virtually wiped out in countries such as the United States, Canada, and Australia. In terms of this view, the white settlers of South Africa found here primitive pagan people who knew no wheeled transport, no writing, no system of market exchange — not even a notation of time. In their view Western civilization brought peace from tribal warfare, Christianity, education, social order, medicine, and economic progress.

Defying the current emphasis on human rights and equality for all in the rest of the Western world, many white South Africans, in the tradition of earlier times, take economic and educational inequality for granted. This does not mean that white South Africans are basically morally different from Americans or Europeans; but only that public opinion in South Africa has not yet caught up with these countries. In the United States a feeling of responsibility for the poor is a fairly

Stratification, Inequality and Conflict

recent development and there are still many conservative Americans who believe the poor are simply lazy and have to work harder to improve their own lot.

In contrast to contemporary Western thought, many white South Africans still do not approve of attempts by whites to assist blacks in educational, economic, and social development. Ideas of one's own race being different, of one's responsibility to one's own people, of the duty of blacks to return to their own people to help them, have been cultivated intensively over past decades. Many whites see the advancement of blacks as being the blacks' own responsibility, and regard assistance by whites as favours done out of goodwill.

Few people in responsible positions today would claim publicly that whites are inherently superior to blacks but a subconscious, if not conscious, sense of superiority underlies both the attitudes and the behaviour of most whites.

In contrast to the functionalists the conflict-oriented politicians and academics are acutely aware of the injustice and exploitation in South African society, the intense animosity between the races, and the inevitability of racial conflict under the present circumstances. According to critics of the government, the social and political structure of South Africa, based on racial discrimination, is in itself a denial of all primary ethical concepts. For that reason they do not see the government as legitimately representing even the whites. The South African government is seen as hostile to the interests of the whole community — the exact opposite of what a democratic government should be.

P.L. van den Berghe describes South Africa as an example *par excellence* of what he calls a 'plural society'. He regards the South African situation as an obvious application of the Hegelian dialectic in which change is bound to be abrupt, qualitative and revolutionary, and where conflict is fostered. White domination is the 'major source of conflict and is calling forth its opposite and is sowing the seeds of its own destruction. . . White supremacy is busily digging its own grave in many ways other than ideological. . . South Africa, and, more generally, pluralistic societies, call for a model of change which gives conflict, contradiction, revolution and malintegration a prominent place' (1965: 278-81).

I have already argued for a synthesis between the contrasting one-dimensional interpretations of the stratification system. Obviously we are also in need of a synthesis between the functional and conflict approaches. But before turning to the management of conflict we need to have proper knowledge of the full range of manifestations of conflict in South Africa. This is put forward in Chapter 3.

Chapter three

Manifestations of Conflict and Violence

In Chapter 2 it was argued that the causes of conflict are multidimensional. So are its manifestations. In this chapter I outline some of the major and ongoing manifestations of conflict in South Africa. These include the various manifestations of 'grand' and 'petty' apartheid based on race discrimination and the government's attempts to control and defuse the issue of political rights for the coloured, Indian, and African population groups. The escalation of overt violence is discussed, including political repression and militarization, political protest, and township violence. Certain areas of protest and confrontation are highlighted: the revolt in education, consumer protests and boycotts, labour relations, and the clash between church and state.

Race discrimination: 'grand' and 'petty' apartheid

The word 'apartheid' as such indicates separation. The introduction of the principle of apartheid originated in European colonial policy over time. Several discriminatory laws were passed by the British colonial powers. When the National Party came into power in 1948 they introduced new measures such as the Prohibition of Mixed Marriages Act, the Population Registration Act, the Group Areas Act and, in subsequent years, numerous acts enforcing rigid racial separation.

Full citizenship and political rights for Africans are the most fundamental and crucial issues in South African politics.

In this section I deal with those manifestations of this basic issue which are flashpoints and which generate conflict:

the homelands policy of geographic separation,
mass relocation of Africans,
restrictions on urbanization and influx control,
housing shortages and squatter crises, and
the constitutional crisis.

Manifestations of Conflict and Violence

All these manifestations of conflict arise from the government's refusal to grant Africans full political rights and its attempts to control their movements within South Africa or, in an indirect way, in their homelands. There are six 'self-governing' homelands of which KwaZulu is the best known and four independent states: Transkei, Bophuthatswana, Venda and Ciskei, usually referred to as the TBVC countries. The population of these four TBVC countries amounts to about 6 million. Underlying this policy various forces are at work: race prejudice, economic greed, desire for political power and control, and ideology.

The 'homeland' policy originated as part of the grand apartheid design for complete racial separation. This ideology has been losing its motivating power and therefore both the *raison d'être* and the justification for homelands are falling away. They are no longer a major item on government platforms but their economic and political implications remain major sources and manifestations of conflict.

Homeland incomes are inadequate. The incomes of many homelands residents are, however, supplemented by the earnings of migrant workers and this often makes the difference between starvation and survival. Thus the major part of the income 'earned' by the homeland population is generated in other parts of South Africa. Because homeland economies cannot provide employment for more than a fraction of their working-age populations, this dependence is increasing. The growth in the number of homeland-based Africans who take employment in outside areas is accelerating.

Although the homeland areas are a failure economically and not viable, the homeland policy is still being pursued for political reasons. By giving Africans political rights in the independent or semi-independent homelands, the Government argues that it is morally justified in depriving them of political rights in the remainder of South Africa. This policy gave rise to deprivation and restrictions on movement which were especially evident in mass relocations, restrictions on urbanization, and the refusal to allow shelter for African families in the urban areas.

Mass removals of about 3 million Africans have taken place; having Africans geographically concentrated deprives them of political rights. The removal policy is motivated by grand apartheid ideology, white greed for land, and white determination to exercise political control over Africans. Resettlement has forced many Africans to leave established communities which were logistically viable, and to begin life anew amid environments that were usually located far from urban centres and employment opportunities. The new 'housing' has sometimes consisted of tents or corrugated iron huts, while sanitation facilities and water supplies have been primitive or nonexistent. Some resettlement areas lack schools and clinics. The millions of relocated Africans are left impoverished and embittered.

Although the government stated in 1985 that it would desist from forced removals, some 2 million people were still under threat of removal (SAIRR 1985: 329). The removal strategy became increasingly sophisticated — fewer people were trucked out and dumped in the fields. There were new official catch phrases such as 'removal for development', 'urban renewal' and 'voluntary removal'.

Since the abolition of influx control in 1986, forced removals have been carried out in terms of the Prohibition of Illegal Squatting Act. The pattern has been to de-proclaim townships, declare unwanted Africans as squatters, give them notice to vacate, and then move them to an area selected by the government.

Urbanization is a world-wide phenomenon, which generally occurs with the development of industrialization. In South Africa the discovery of minerals initiated a wave of African urbanization because of the wages offered in the cities and because of taxation measures used to coerce people to join the labour market. Later, restrictions placed on African agriculture (through measures such as the Land Act of 1913) served to limit the amount of land available for African farming, forcing many people into the cities in search of a livelihood.

The flow of Africans to the cities was not, however, permitted to occur freely. There has been a consistent series of attempts over time to stem and even turn the tide of urbanization. This duality in government policy became known as the 'push-pull policy' which has had a marked effect on the nature of urban development in South Africa.

By 1982, 53 per cent of the South African population of 24 milion was urbanized. This included six million Africans and four million whites. It is estimated that 75 per cent of the total African population of South Africa will be urbanized by the year 2000, and that means an increase in the cities of at least 21 million (Dewar, Todes, and Watson 1982: 101). As a result of the geographical movement of all population groups more than half the population of our cities today consists of Africans and only 30 per cent of whites. In spite of this the government has until recently referred to South Africa's major cities as 'white'.

Throughout the world attempts have been made from time to time to limit urban growth but in South Africa these attempts have been blatantly racist. Thus while the importance of African labour to urban industrial development has been recognized, it is also known that political control of the cities could be lost if the urbanization of Africans is not kept to a minimum. A vast, complex and intricate system of influx control machinery had therefore to be developed, with migrant labour as its essential cornerstone.

In 1985 a major change in government policy occurred. It was announced that a uniform identity document would be issued to all population groups and that citizens of the 'independent' homelands who resided permanently in 'South Africa' were to have their South African citizenship restored in the form of dual citizenship. In July 1986 influx control was formally abolished. While the government has accepted the permanence of 'resident' Africans in the common areas of South Africa and allowed more freedom of movement in the urban areas, doubts about exact legal status and civil rights remain.

Problems relating to urbanization remain and generate major manifestations of conflict. No government in the world could dispossess the majority of its citizens and confine them to over-populated rural reserves without inviting resistance. Only in the late 1980s did the government admit that Africans were entitled to representation in the central government. This is discussed below.

The lack of adequate housing for all black people, but especially for Africans, has resulted in serious overcrowding and squatting. Changing government policies relating to Africans and squatter settlements led to uncertainty regarding the permanence of occupation in such settlements, and therefore 'normal' upgrading did not take place. This led to ever worsening conditions. The cruel demolition of the only homes people have, especially in winter, has caused great bitterness among squatters. In 1987, the National Building Institute estimated that the black housing backlog outside the homelands might be as high as 832,000 units. In October 1987, the Minister of Constitutional Development and Planning estimated that over 1.2 million people were squatting in South Africa (*Cape Times*, 29 October 1987). According to the Black Sash, at least five million people — one in every six South Africans — are homeless (*Weekly Mail*, 13-19 November 1987).

The government is quick to point out that since it abolished influx control in 1986 anyone can come to a city to look for work. But individuals are not allowed to remain in cities unless they have state-approved housing. Such housing is not available. More and more people are setting up informal settlements on apparently unoccupied land, only to be arrested for trespassing or squatting.

The amended Illegal Squatting Act provides for the summary eviction of 'persons unlawfully occupying land', demolition of unlawful structures, and exorbitant penalties for offenders. The Trespass Act has a maximum penalty of a R2,000 fine and two years' imprisonment (*Weekly Mail*, 13-19 November 1987).

Frustration over extremely poor living conditions is an important flashpoint for unrest. Nation-wide rent boycotts have occurred in African townships, mainly as a protest against poor conditions. These boycotts remain a continuing source of violence as the authorities try to evict residents and residents resist.

Events surrounding South African constitutional development over the last decade disclose the multi-dimensional nature of conflict. The impetus for constitutional reform was born in the wake of the Soweto riots of 1976 and the simultaneous report of the Theron Commission, appointed by the government, to inquire into and report on the coloured peoples' progress since 1960 and to make recommendations on future development. The commission recommended, *inter alia*, that a number of radical constitutional adjustments should be considered as a matter of urgent public interest.

As a result of these internal discussions and increasing international pressures for constitutional reform, the Nationalist government appointed a parliamentary Select Committee and then the Schlebusch Commission, which in turn recommended the creation of a President's Council to advise the government on further constitutional development. This process culminated in a constitutional referendum (for white voters only) in November 1983. Sixty-six per cent of the white electorate accepted constitutional proposals which created an executive state president with extensive powers, and a tri-cameral, racially based legislature — a departure from the Westminster pattern. Coloured and Indian legislative bodies were established but Africans were excluded from the new constitutional dispensation. The government's reason was that those Africans living in 'white South Africa' should exercise their political rights in their respective homelands.

This 'power-sharing' tri-cameral constitution was implemented in September 1984 after elections in the coloured and Indian communities. It sparked the formation of the United Democratic Front (UDF) in August 1983, precipitated the violence that swept across the country towards the end of 1984 (leading eventually to the imposition of the first State of Emergency in mid-1985), and split the white communities, both Afrikaner and English, down the middle.

The exit of Andries Treurnicht and sixteen other MPs from the National Party (NP) in February 1982, and the subsequent creation of the Conservative Party (CP) broke down the ethnic core of Afrikanerdom. Right-wing objections were based on the assumption that the apparent power sharing of the constitution would inevitably lead to black 'majority rule' and domination in a unitary state. This split in political Afrikanerdom (the CP and far-right Herstigte Nasionale Party voting 'no' in the constitutional referendum, the NP 'yes') was a harbinger of the 1987 religious schism which took place in the Dutch Reformed Church (DRC).

The proposed constitutional reform also led to conflict amongst English-speaking whites. The predominantly English-speaking and liberal Progressive Federal Party (PFP), then still the official parliamentary opposition, advocated a 'no' vote in the constitutional referendum. It has been estimated, however, that as many as 60 per cent of PFP supporters voted against the party line — accepting the *bona fides* of the government's 'step in the right direction' argument.

Many prominent English-speaking businessmen put forward a 'yes' vote, while a fringe minority of whites became active in the anti-tricameral constitution campaign, spearheaded by the newly-formed UDF. More violent forms of conflict related to the new constitution arose in the black communities, especially after the formation of extra-parliamentary organizations such as the UDF and the National Forum (NF), which aimed at destroying the tri-cameral constitution and urged Indians and coloured people to boycott the elections for tri-cameral representatives. The boycott strategy of the extra-parliamentary organizations was relatively successful as country-wide polls of only 17.6 per cent and 16.2 per cent of potential (as opposed to registered) voters were recorded for the coloured House of Representatives and the Indian House of Delegates respectively. Even the traditionally more pragmatic Inkatha, the national cultural liberation movement, rejected the new constitution outright. But just as it is false to overlook white opposition (both liberal and racist) to the constitution, it is wrong to assume unified black opposition. The coloured Labour Party precipitated the demise of the Black Alliance with Inkatha by entering the tri-cameral system against all expectation. There were allegedly minority elements within the UDF who favoured 'destruction from within'. Archie Gumede, one of three presidents of the UDF, has expressed such sentiments on various occasions.

The inadequacy of the tri-cameral system and the resultant constitutional crisis are highlighted by the increasing repression and counter-violence that the country has experienced since September 1984. As early as 1983 a Special Cabinet Committee (SCC) was appointed 'to investigate the constitutional position of Africans, particularly those living outside the homelands' (SAIRR 1985: 61). The Government has admitted that the exclusion of Africans from constitutional structures requires urgent attention, but the responsible minister categorically denied that a fourth chamber for Africans is being considered. Establishment of a non-statutory forum, aimed at supplementing the activities of the SCC, was announced in January 1985, but did not get off the ground. A statutory forum, the National Statutory Council (NSC), represented the next government initiative, but its failure to attract any credible black spokesmen creates an ongoing impasse. Even the usually relatively 'moderate' Zulu leader, Chief Mangosuthu Buthelezi, has rejected all Government overtures seeking his participation in the NSC. So has the urban African leader Steve Kgame of the Urban Councils' Association of South Africa (UCASA). Both these men, and the majority of the homeland leaders, reiterate the basic demands usually associated with the extra-parliamentary organizations — release of all political prisoners and detainees (including Mandela), troops out of the townships and an ending of the State of Emergency. There does not seem to be any strong prospect of credible black leaders participating in the council until the Government is prepared to abandon group areas and race classification.

In an attempt to break the current constitutional deadlock, the Inkatha-dominated KwaZulu government and the New Republic Party (NRP), which controlled the Natal Provincial Council at the time, jointly convened a 'regional convention' which took place from April to November 1986. Invited members represented a wide range of organizations active in Natal although the left wing — the African National Congress (ANC), the UDF, the Congress of South African Trade Unions (Cosatu), and the Natal Indian Congress — refused to participate. So did the Conservative and Herstigte Nasionale parties on the right. The National Party members attended as observers, not as official delegates.

The Indaba produced a blueprint for a system of non-racial, power-sharing government for KwaZulu and the common areas of Natal. A bill of rights and various democratic mechanisms ensure that neither white nor black authoritarian rule will ensue. Government spokesmen rejected the Indaba proposals before the election in May 1987 on the grounds that it provided insufficient protection for white minorities. However, it has become more receptive since then and an inter-racial joint executive authority for Natal came into being towards the end of 1987. The government has still not agreed to a legislative forum for the area.

In line with its distinction between 'own' and 'general' affairs, in the tri-cameral system, the government has also been active in restructuring local government so that Regional Services Councils could handle matters of common and general concern at regional level. The first eight started operating on 1 July 1987. The government's attempt to defuse the constitutional crisis at the national level by decentralizing power to the regional and local level, is meeting with little success. The dissolution of elected Provincial Councils and the establishment of government-appointed executive authorities in place of representative bodies has also been opposed.

A fundamental flaw in many of the government's regional and national initiatives is the artificial and unworkable distinction between 'own' and 'general' affairs. The concept of 'own' affairs is not a functional option, but a legacy of earlier racist ideology. The implementation of 'own' affairs has become increasingly absurd. One major objection to these new regional and provincial initiatives lies in the fact that elected executives have been replaced by appointed executives. On the positive side, these new regional and provincial authorities are now multi-racial, and include Africans. It is a way of gradually integrating aspects of government by authoritarian measures.

The phrase 'petty apartheid' is normally used to indicate practical measures separating whites and blacks in all walks of life, as distinguished from the grand design of geographic separation of black homelands. Petty apartheid relates to discrimination regarding residential areas, amenities such as cinemas, and restaurants, taxis and public transport, buses, post offices, hospitals, beaches, swimming pools, parks and other amenities.

The principal legal underpinning of residential and business segregation in the urban areas of South Africa is the Group Areas Act. The statute was first enhanced in 1950 and revised in 1957 and in 1966, but it is rooted in a number of pre-1948 laws aimed mainly at the ownership and occupation of land by Indians. The act provides for the creation of separate group areas in towns and cities for whites, Africans, coloured people, and Indians. The Group Areas Act has severe discriminatory consequences.

Over the years a total of 126,176 families have been declared 'disqualified' because of their racial classification and forced to move from their homes under the Group Areas Act. Of these families, 2,418 (2 per cent) were white, 83,691 (66 per cent) were coloured, and 40,067 (32 per cent) were Indian (*Weekly Mail*, 25-31 July 1987). The forced removal of Africans occurs under other laws discussed earlier.

The negative impact of the Group Areas Act has been a major cause of bitterness in South Africa and this has been confirmed by one government commission of enquiry after another. Community groups are destroyed and friends and neighbours are lost. The effect of legally enforced segregation has been to change the face of our cities. Control over the developed commercial and industrial areas and all desirable suburbs has been consolidated in white hands as other groups have been moved to distant sites.

Political repression and militarization

Revolutions do not occur in open democratic societies. Political protest, violence and civil war in South Africa arise in reaction to political repression and to the denial of free political expression and participation in decision making by black people in South Africa. Security legislation in itself constitutes a source of conflict and violence.

Political repression is one form of institutional violence and its significance can only be fully understood when seen in conjunction with the unequal and plural nature of South African society. Plural societies are prone to instability and violence, especially when traditional patterns of life are disrupted and uneducated masses are drawn into a modern economy and demand higher standards of living.

Legal forms of repression exist under the widely defined security laws, political trials and states of emergency declared under the Public Safety Act of 1953. The State is legally entitled to ban gatherings and meetings, to ban organizations, to ban and restrict persons, to list people so that they may not be quoted, to restrict travel and withhold visas, and to detain people without trial.

The two best known political organizations banned by the government are the African National Congress (ANC) and the Pan Africanist Congress (PAC). The leaders of these organizations are either serving long-term prison sentences or live in exile.

In terms of emergency powers, restrictions on funerals were proclaimed, curfews and control over non-residents of an area came into effect, the media were severely restricted, and information suppressed.

In 1984, 1,149 people were detained under security legislation. This figure grew to some 10,000 in 1985, of whom 7,361 were held under emergency regulations. In the year beginning 12 June 1986, when the second emergency was declared, at least 25,000 people were detained (*Weekly Mail*, 5 June 1987). During 1986 there were at least seven detention-related deaths (*Weekly Mail*, 13–19 February 1987).

The Detainees' Parents' Support Committee (DPSC) has listed court applications involving seventy-five applicants relating to allegations of assault and torture of security and emergency detainees.

The best known study of alleged torture is the so-called 'Torture Report' (Foster 1987). This study reported on personal interviews with a representative sample of 176 former security detainees. The vast majority claimed to have been subjected to both physical and psychological torture. The average detainee claimed to have been subjected to ten different forms of torture.

Since 1984, South African state and domestic politics have become increasingly militarized; executive/military government rather than parliamentary government has become more prominent. In 1986 the government established the low-profile National Security Management System, dominated by the security forces.

The South African Defence Force (SADF) has been deployed in South Africa's townships as part of the strategy of political repression. The withdrawal of troops enforcing 'law and order' in black areas has been demanded time and again by community organizations and political groupings. The use of conscripts in suppressing political protest has also led to growing unease among young white males, some of whom have refused to serve in the SADF as a result.

Political protest violence

The terms 'cycle of violence' or 'spiral of violence' have become part of the South African political lexicon. Institutional violence by the state leads to violent reactions and protest and insurgent violence escalates.

Government opponents feel more and more justified in resorting to political violence and so the government feels justified in maintaining the national state of emergency. This escalation of political violence has been cited by the government as the major reason for the declarations of various states of emergency over the past few years. Apart from the major periods of civil unrest in 1976, 1980, and 1984, there has been a steady increase in incidents of political protest violence. The government has attributed this escalation to the explicit policy of the revolutionary forces to overthrow the government.

On 12 June 1986 the State President declared the Second National State of Emergency. In a government publication, *The National State of Emergency* (South Africa Bureau for Information 1987), the 'rising spiral of unrest, instigated primarily by Black consciousness and other radical groups' was cited. The government argued that the ANC sought to capitalize on this situation and referred in this connection to Oliver Tambo's major policy speech on 8 January 1986 in which he stated that the ANC would continue to make South Africa ungovernable, would build its forces into a massive army of liberation, and would escalate its resolute military offensive.

When the National State of Emergency was declared three objectives were set:

- The restoration of law and order and security
- A return to normality in the unrest-ravaged black residential areas.
- The creation of a climate in which constitutional change could take place.

When the government renewed the state of emergency in February 1988, the following figures were released by the Minister of Law and Order to the Sunday paper *Rapport* (28 February 1988): In the years 1977 to 1980, there were never more than twenty terrorist acts per year. Since then these figures have escalated rapidly: there were 58 in 1981, 39 in 1982, 56 in 1983, 44 in 1984, 136 in 1985, 230 in 1986 and 234 in 1987.

In the publication of the South Africa Bureau for Information, *The National State of Emergency* (1987: 2) the government listed the following incidences of unrest in the twenty months between September 1984 and May 1986:

- 3,477 private black houses badly damaged or destroyed;
- 1,220 schools badly damaged or destroyed;
- over 7,000 buses and 10,000 other vehicles damaged or destroyed.

According to the South African Institute of Race Relations the number of fatalities since the political violence erupted in September 1984 amounted to 680 from September 1984 to August 1985 and 1,520 from September 1985 to August 1986, a total of 2,200 in two years. The actual number of political deaths in the last period could be higher than the statistics indicate, since the emergency regulations restrict press coverage and make it difficult to obtain reliable information. There are, nevertheless, clear indications that political deaths have greatly decreased during the periods of emergency.

At the end of 1983, when detailed information was available from various sources, the Centre for Intergroup Studies undertook an analysis of acts of physical violence of a political nature or committed for political reasons, i.e. either to maintain the *status quo* or to bring about change (Van der Merwe and Hendricks 1983). The period covered was from the end of the Soweto disturbances in January 1977 until May 1983, the occasion of the bomb blast in Pretoria and the subsequent attack on Maputo by the South African Defence Force.

We recorded 236 incidents over the period. Most incidents resulted in structural damage, injury, and death. We have recorded details of these incidents in terms of the parties responsible, the nature of the act, and the type of victims.

Table 1 shows that the ANC was responsible for eighty incidents causing damage to property, the right wing for eighteen, and the government for four. Damage was caused in nine additional incidents where the responsible parties were not identified. The government was responsible for ninety-eight deaths, the ANC for fifty-two, and the right wing for one. Another thirty-one deaths were caused by unidentified parties. In some cases deaths were caused by responsible parties in their own ranks. Injuries were caused to 286 people by the ANC, to 125 people by unidentified parties, to forty-eight people by the government and to two people by the right wing.

All incidents were classified in terms of the following four broad categories: (a) intended/attempted violence; aborted actions; (b) structural damage caused; (c) injury caused to human beings; and (d) deaths resulting from the act.

We also classified human victims in terms of four categories: (a) military, police and guerilla fighters; (b) paramilitary staff and employees such as staff of courts of law, Administration Boards, power plants and railways; (c) civilians injured or killed in attacks aimed primarily at military and paramilitary structures or personnel; and (d) civilians injured or killed deliberately. Structural damage to property was classified in a similar way.

In sixty-seven incidents there was evidence of intended violence but no damage or injury resulted. In 121 incidents structural damage was caused. In fifty-five incidents 461 people were injured, and in a further fifty-five incidents 167 people were killed.

Table 1 Parties responsible for damage, injury, or death

	Government			Right wing			ANC			Other		
	Incident	People		Incident	People		Incident	People		Incident	People	
	Damage	Injury	Death	Damage	Injury	Death	Damage	Injury	Death	Damage	Injury	Death
1977			2		1		8	12	5	4	20	—
1978			3	4	1	1	3	7	6	1	3	1
1979			1	5			4	9	3	1	3	1
1980	1	5	6	7			8	16	3	5	4	6
1981	1		31	1			33	22	13	7	8	4
1982	1	1	46	1			16	6	1	1	2	3
1983	1	42	9				8	214	21		87	1
	4	48	98	18	2	1	80	286	52	19	125	15

Altogether 628 people were injured or killed in this period, more than half of them during 1983. If we look at the number of people affected period by period, there appears to be a trend. For the years 1977, 1978 and 1979 a total of seventy-nine people were affected (injured or killed); for the years 1980, 1981 and 1982, the total figure rose to 175; and in the first five months of 1983 the total figure amounted to 374. Of the total of 628 people affected, 151 were military or police staff, 29 were from paramilitary institutions and 448 were civilians. The majority of civilians affected (392) were victims of attacks that were aimed at or were associated with military and paramilitary targets. Fifty-six civilians were deliberately killed or injured.

The largest number of civilians deliberately affected resulted from the Carlton bomb incident in Johannesburg in 1977; the largest number affected by an attack associated with a military target was in the Pretoria bomb blast in May 1983.

The intensity of the conflict, the extent of bitterness and hatred, and the thirst for revenge were reflected in the attitudes towards the suffering of civilians. Both the Government and the ANC have indicated the inevitability of civilian deaths. In an editorial comment (22 November 1983) the South African Broadcasting Corporation warned: 'When South Africa involves itself in pre-emptive or punitive strikes the governments of these (neighbouring) countries must not complain when the innocent suffer as a consequence.'

ANC supporters have argued that it is not possible to distinguish between military and civilians among South African whites, especialy in rural areas, because all farmers are armed. Attacks on farming families are seen as guerilla action.

In South Africa we have not experienced deliberate attacks on civilian whites to the same extent as in Northern Ireland and in the Middle East. But there is every indication that the longer the internal unrest continues the greater become the chances that such attacks will increase. There has already been an increase in deliberate attacks on civilians, especially on blacks participating in the system: African trade union leaders and African, Indian and coloured politicians, both conservative and radical.

At the beginning of 1988 the Minister of Law and Order maintained that the targets of the ANC and PAC switched during 1985, 1986 and 1987 from buildings to people (*Rapport*, 28 February 1988). According to the article in *Rapport* the main targets of the ANC since 1976 have been civilians and civil servants who were not members of the security forces: 37 per cent of recorded incidents were murders or attempted murders of such people. The second main targets have been policemen (30 per cent). Other targets were: railway property (10%); state and public buildings (8%); and power installations (7%).

The Minister said that the percentage of civilian victims had increased from 37 per cent in 1986 to 42 per cent in 1987. He also explained the Security Forces had arrested, wounded, or killed 531 'terrorists and collaborators' in 1987 alone.

Township violence

In 1985 a new phenomenon began to receive media attention — what came to be known as 'black-on-black' violence. This violence has led to a state of near-anarchy involving a wide range of antagonistic groups and innocent victims. The major conflict has been waged between groups willing to operate within the socio-economic system and those who refuse, described in Chapter 4 as the intra- and extra-systematic opposition groups. The eruption of township violence has had one particularly horrific aspect: the 'necklace' method of killing, whereby a petrol filled tyre is put around the victim's body and then set alight.

According to the South Africa Bureau for Information (1987: 2,9), 573 deaths were due to 'black-on-black' violence of whom 295 were killed by the 'necklace' between September 1984 and May 1986. Between 1 January 1986 and 4 April 1987, 484 people were burnt to death of whom 210 were killed by the 'necklace'.

Another form of 'black-on-black' violence which has become prominent in recent years takes the form of 'extralegal violence by right-wing vigilantes' (Haysom 1986: 1). Four distinct types of vigilante groups operating in South Africa can be identified:

- Groups linked to community councillors wishing to protect themselves and their families and homes against violent attacks, retain control of their areas, and protect their patronage.
- Groups in several homelands that have operated since the beginning of the decade, 'working either with passive connivance of the homeland authorities or under their direct instructions'.
- Groups formed to restore 'law and order' in particular areas.
- Groups in coloured and Indian areas which emerged when these communities believed themselves to be under attack from neighbouring African areas.

Despite the diverse reasons for the formation of the vigilante groups, their attacks were primarily directed at 'anti-government militants' (SAIRR 1985: 551). Allegations of security force collusion with vigilantes are often made.

The Minister of Law and Order was sued for R312,000 by the Methodist Church and twenty-one squatter families in Cape Town who lost their homes in May and June 1986. The plaintiffs allege that the South African Police actively assisted in, or did nothing to prevent, the destruction of their homes in June 1986 by a local vigilante group, the so-called Witdoeke. Some 3,198 similar cases involving Crossroads and squatter families, with claims of over R5 million, are pending. Haysom (1986: 7) says the emergence of vigilantes should be seen in the context of a crisis of control in black areas. He sees the operation of groups of vigilantes as an attempt to alter the balance of power in townships.

> Disorganisation of the community is essentially what vigilante activity is about. A disorganised and cowed community provides a vacuum for community councils, development boards or homeland authorities to fill and on which they may impose their will. This is so particularly for black communities who are without access to direct political power and who have only organisation as their weapon.
>
> (Haysom 1986: 11)

Violence committed between opposing political groups within the broader anti-apartheid movement has become widespread. The most significant clashes in this category took place between UDF affiliated groups and the Azanian Peoples Organisation (Azapo) in the Eastern Cape, and between Inkatha and the UDF in Natal.

In Natal the situation is particularly severe. UDF and Cosatu allegations of violence against Inkatha members and corresponding counter-allegations have become an everyday occurrence. August 1985 saw the eruption of large scale and devastating violence in the greater Durban area. Many people were killed and families were left homeless. Violence has increased steadily since then and hundreds of people have been killed. Although leaders have expressed themselves willing to end the fighting, there appears to have been a complete breakdown in communication with the rank-and-file membership. The detention of prominent UDF leaders during crucial negotiations also contributed to the lack of progress towards resolving the violence.

Assassinations of a number of prominent anti-government people are widely believed to have been politically motivated. Victims include Mrs Victoria Mxenge, a human rights lawyer, Mr Balandwa Ndondo, a former Students' Representative Council president, and Mr Mathew Goniwe, active in the Cradock Residents' Association.

Another township flashpoint has been created with the issuing of arms to special constables, better known as 'kits-konstabels'. These constables, drawn from the black community, are provided with only three months' training and are then issued with arms. Guns issued to special constables have been used to commit at least 95 crimes in Cape Province and Transvaal up to September 1987 (figures released by Minister of Law and Order, Adriaan Vlok, in Parliament).

Revolt in education

Since the 1976 Soweto uprisings, education has been a hot political issue. A deep, simmering dissatisfaction with the national political system and with what has become known as 'gutter education' has become the fuel for violence.

In late 1984, black school pupils started a nationwide campaign against inadequate education which led to a punitive response and then to school boycotts. By the end of the year the boycotts had affected most parts of the country. The disturbances continued in 1985. Issues that set off boycotts in different schools varied but some uniform demands were made throughout the country: the lifting of the state of emergency, the removal of the South African Police and the South African Defence Force from townships, the teaching of 'peoples' education' in schools, and the release of detainees. Two significant new features of the boycotts were the extensive participation by coloured pupils and the high degree of cooperation between pupils and their parents.

According to the Department of Education and Training (DET) 674,275 African pupils at 907 schools were affected by boycotts in 1985. About 360,000 coloured pupils were affected. An important student organization and UDF affiliate, the Congress of South African Students (COSAS) was banned in this year. Another significant development was the Soweto Parents Crisis Committee's conference in December 1985 in Johannesburg, which led to the formation of the National Education Crisis Committee (NECC).

Delegates to this conference clearly realized that they had to tackle the education crisis head-on if they wanted to prevent 1986 becoming 'The Year of No Schooling' (Zille 1987: 25). The return to schools was therefore presented to students as 'a tactical shift to advance their struggle'. In March 1986 the NECC went even further in calling on students to 're-occupy' the schools. According to Zille a pivotal change of strategy took place.

> At a time when the gulf between the government and the resistance movements seemed to have become entirely unbridgeable, an area of meaningful consensus emerged . . . Both the government and its most important political antagonists (including the ANC) agreed on the major parameters: not only should education continue, but it should proceed within the institutional base of the schools.
>
> (Zille 1987: 26)

But the opportunity for serious negotiations addressing the students' grievances was lost. The government re-declared a state of emergency and detained as many NECC leaders as it could find. By August 1986, 20 per cent of DET pupils had been barred from school for refusing to register or carry identity cards (*Weekly Mail*, 1-7 August 1986).

The disruptions at South Africa's schools point to 'a continuing unresolved conflict, which is likely to be repeated for there is no indication that the political fundamentals at the heart of the protests are to be changed' (van den Berg and O'Connell 1986: 8).

The demand for non-racial, democratic and anti-capitalist 'people's education' is likely to continue to grow, leading to a kind of stalemate. Under the leadership of the able Chairman of the national Education Crisis Committee (NECC), Mr Vusi Khanyile, the protesting groups took significant steps to break the deadlock by initiating negotiations with the authorities. These initiatives came to an effective halt when Khanyile was detained without trail in December 1986.

Consumer protests and boycott

Consumer action has become a widespread tactic in South Africa in recent years. It takes many forms, the most common being boycotts of white businesses in support of local and national demands by opposition groups, rent boycotts in protest against conditions in the townships, and boycotts of specific businesses or products because of particular worker grievances. 'Consumer boycotts of white businesses resulted in unprecedented local-level negotiations between the authorities, businessmen, unions, and township organisations' (SAIRR 1985: 555).

Some boycotts had substantial community backing but others were imposed by coercion. Most boycotts were organized by UDF affiliates, although National Forum Committee (NFC) affiliates and other independent political groupings played a role. Local boycott committees generally consisted of representatives of unions and of community and youth organizations. The boycotts brought together workers, students, church people, businessmen, and rural people in practical action against the government and its policies.

The organizations involved in boycotts did not always have a shared vision of the role and the potential of the boycott weapon. There were also problems with unilateral boycott declarations, especially by the UDF. In 1985 the UDF launched consumer boycotts in Johannesburg, Pretoria, Port Elizabeth, East London, and the Western Cape without consulting other organizations first.

The effects of consumer boycotts varied vastly from area to area. In some places shops had to close and others experienced drops of up to eighty per cent in sales. In other areas the impact was barely noticeable. The most effective was the Port Elizabeth boycott which lasted from 15 July to 1 December 1985. It was called off only after extensive negotiations between the Port Elizabeth Chamber of Commerce and the boycott spokesperson, Mr Mkhuseli Jack.

One of the most important effects of the boycotts was that a new politics of negotiation emerged. However, police detained many of the original boycott organizers, closed some black-owned shops, and put pressure on wholesalers not to supply black-owned shops with goods. In Fort Beaufort police closed black-owned shops and detained their owners under the emergency regulations (SAIRR 1985: 559). Thus police action often undermined the newly established politics of negotiation.

Another form of consumer protest that has become widespread is protest against public transport. Economic and political deprivation coincide. The bus owners are private capitalist monopolies subsidised by the apartheid government. Buses, like government buildings, beer halls and schools, are symbols of inequality and oppression. Buses are there to transport people to and from areas where they are forced to live by the government.

Public transport services are controlled by the National Transport Commission, which strengthens the impression of collusion between the government and the owners. Black commuters are not represented on this commission or on the boards of directors of these companies, and are thus denied control over conditions, time tables, or fares.

Since they have limited resources, the only worthwhile political action open to commuters is that of consumer action. In 1986, bus boycotts took place on the West Rand and in Duduza, Soweto, and Lebowa. Frustration over the issue of public transport simmers just below the surface and erupts regularly, frequently resulting in physical violence. Buses, as symbols of oppression, have become the targets of sabotage and stone throwing. PUTCO, the major Johannesburg company, lost R28 million between August 1984 and March 1986 as a result of township unrest (SAIRR 1986: 206).

In 1987 trains in the South African Transport Services (SATS) (even more closely identified with the government) became targets of sabotage as a side-effect of labour strikes. In the eight months leading up to April 1986, train windows in the Cape Peninsula were shattered at a rate of more than 500 a month in stoning incidents.

Labour relations

Strikes were the most visible manifestations of conflict between management and labour. Between January and March 1973 a series of strikes by unregistered unions over low wages broke out in Durban. From then on a new trend developed with demands for union recognition and establishment of negotiating channels becoming as important as wage demands. As the labour movement grew stronger, grievances became more sophisticated. Challenges to management were posed around issues of unfair dismissals and unilateral or arbitrary actions by management.

In 1979 South Africa entered into a new labour dispensation. Proposals by a commission of inquiry into labour legislation, under the chairmanship of Nic Wiehahn, became law officially recognizing African trade unions. Trade union membership of African and non-racial unions has grown dramatically since.

At the end of 1985 a new non-racial federation, the Congress of South African Trade Unions (Cosatu), emerged as the largest trade union federation in South Africa. After five years of complex and difficult negotiations, Cosatu has succeeded in uniting thirty-three of the diverse newer unions, with a paid-up membership of nearly 450,000 workers.

The other federation is the National Council of Trade Unions (Nactu) which came into existence after the merger of CUSA and AZACTU. Its policy differs from Cosatu's in that it is black consciousness orientated and espouses the principle of 'anti-racism'. Nactu has twenty-three affiliates and claims 248,000 paid-up and 420,000 signed-up members.

Because the majority of the population is denied the franchise and other human rights many black workers have come to view the union movement as an important political vehicle. The government has acted severely against unionists suspected of 'political' activity. Trade unions, and especially those affiliated to Cosatu, have been hard hit by detentions under the Internal Security Act, the Emergency regulations, the Criminal Procedures Act, the Intimidation Act, and other regulations. Eighty-three per cent of all the union leaders detained in the 1986 emergency crackdown were from Cosatu.

Trade union offices have become targets of bombings, fires, and destruction. The most notable of these were the two blasts that ripped through Cosatu House, Johannesburg, in May 1987, causing serious structural damage and leaving Cosatu with a R1 million repair bill. Community House in Cape Town, housing Cosatu offices as well as church groups was bombed soon after its completion, and other trade union offices throughout the country have been targets of wilful destruction.

Inter-union rivalry has also exacted its toll. In response to the threat posed to Inkatha by the organizational strength of Cosatu, it formed its own trade union on 1 May 1986, the United Workers Union of South Africa (Uwusa). The major difference between it and Cosatu or Nactu lies in Uwusa's orientation towards capitalism. It is committed to 'liberating the free enterprise system from racist apartheid control and making it a vehicle for progress'.

Ever since the Uwusa launch tension between it and Cosatu has been rife. The general secretary of Uwusa accused Cosatu of hijacking workers and Chief Buthelezi accused Cosatu of taking orders from the ANC and 'orchestrating an international campaign against Inkatha' (SAIRR 1986: 245). The animosity between Cosatu and Uwusa eventually spilled over into violence. Accusations abound and union officials have been subject to attacks and counter attacks. Several restraining interdicts were granted by the courts.

Church-state confrontation

Another manifestation of the conflict in South Africa is the confrontation between the Christian churches and the government. The South African Council of Churches (SACC), which includes the non-racial mainline Protestant churches, churches of the Lutheran and Dutch Reformed traditions and a number of African churches, has been one of the more outspoken anti-apartheid groups within South Africa. Its international links through the World Council of Churches (WCC) have made it one of the government's more effective critics and it has accordingly borne the brunt of severe state repression. This has been especially marked over the last few years as increased polarization has occurred, with the subsequent weakening of the liberal 'moderate' centre in South African politics. Church workers have been regularly included in lists of detainees and the SACC, like other liberal groupings, has been progressively pushed left. In 1985 the annual national conference of the SACC called on foreign churches to promote disinvestment and similar economic measures as a means to facilitate 'peaceful' but nonetheless fundamental change in South Africa. Prominent church leaders such as Bishop Manas Buthelezi, Nobel Prize winner Desmond Tutu, Dr Allan Boesak, and Dr Beyers Naude are outspoken critics of the apartheid government. The result is intensified church-state conflict.

The South African Catholic Bishops' Conference (SACBC) is another cogent critic of apartheid, and gave general support to the Kairos Document (Kairos Theologians 1985) when it was released in September 1985. The Kairos Document was produced during the height of the crisis at the end of 1985 (Winkler *et al.* 1987: 15). It was subsequently endorsed by others, although Desmond Tutu was a notable 'absentee'. The Reverend Frank Chikane, then head of the Institute of Contextual Theology, was a prominent initiator of and contributor to the document. Chikane, a leading liberation theologian, replaced Beyers Naude as general secretary of the SACC in April 1987. The Kairos Document initiated a widespread and at times vociferous debate. Many church leaders have serious problems with the Kairos Document's implied condonation of certain kinds of violence.

The central tenet of the Kairos Document is its support of the Christian doctrine of the just war and, by extension, the just revolution. In July 1985, Beyers Naude, then general secretary of the SACC, made a speech at a WCC meeting in Harare which was a clear indication of things to come. He is reported to have said that, although all churches in South Africa continued to advocate non-violence, the SACC no longer condemned those who had decided to enter into the violent struggle because of their convictions (*Star*, 11 September 1985).

Those in the South African churches who adopt a universal as opposed to situational or relative pacifist stance have objected to Kairos. To them, justifying liberatory violence (i.e. violent intimidation and the general 'armed struggle') in reaction to the alleged 'structural' violence of apartheid is not only unchristian, but a certain recipe for increased violence and inevitable disaster.

At a meeting of the World Council of Churches in Zambia attended by South African clergy and representatives of the exiled liberation forces — i.e. the African National Congress (ANC), the Pan Africanist Congress (PAC), and the South West African Peoples Organisation (Swapo) - the 'Lusaka' statement was drawn up, which accepted the use of force by these organizations on the same grounds as those set out in the Kairos Document of 1985. In July 1987 the annual national conference of the SACC adopted the Lusaka statement. Outgoing general secretary Beyers Naude stated in his report, 'It is simply not good enough to state that the church is against violence in any form; this has become a platitude which has almost lost its meaning in the situation of increasing conflict, violence and bloodshed' (*Weekly Mail*, 3-9 July 1987). Church leaders are by no means unanimous on the issue of violence and its relationship with liberation. But it is clear that support for the just revolution view will grow. As it does, state-church conflict will escalate.

Discounting the few white theologians who broke from the white 'mother' Dutch Reformed Church and joined the sister DRC coloured and African churches, the mother church has not inaccurately been labelled 'the National Party at prayer'. In fact, it may be argued that by consciously attempting to remain 'above' secular and political matters, the white DRC was often to the right of official government thinking on crucial issues. This was especially so after the 1982 split in the National Party which led to the creation of the far-right Conservative Party — the official opposition in the House of Assembly since May 1987. Realizing that its religious flock was politically divided, especially post-1982, the DRC attempted to avoid the political scene.

None the less, in 1983, the traditionally more liberal Western Cape synod of the DRC was critical of apartheid policy and its 'unchristian consequences'. In October 1986 a resolution adopted at the general synod moved forward considerably. The relevant portion read, 'The conviction has gradually grown that a forced separation and division of peoples cannot be considered a Biblical imperative. The attempt to justify such an injunction as derived from the Bible must be recognised as an error and should be rejected.'

At the same time the General Synod adopted the policy document *Church and Society* which opened the door to racially mixed congregations. In response to these liberal trends within the white DRC a group of ultra-conservative theologians initiated a split from the DRC in mid-1987. The Afrikaanse Protestantse Kerk (APK) was established and soon claimed to have seventy-two congregations and 12,000 members of whom 8,000 were communicants. The DRC admits that 340 elders and 250 deacons left the church but tried to play down this defection by pointing out that APK membership represents only 0.44 per cent of the DRC (*Die Burger*, 25 November 1987). The inter-church conflict between the Afrikaans-language churches will intensify over the short term.

This religious split in Afrikanerdom can also be interpreted as the belated ecumenical response to the Afrikaner party-political split of 1982. The incumbent Moderator of the DRC, Professor Johan Heyns, has led the DRC to a position to the left of the governing National Party. He has in fact stated publicly that if the South African government does not dismantle apartheid completely there will be a church–state clash.

The DRC is inviting a conflict with the state in becoming openly more critical of National Party policy. The 1987 Western Cape Synod of the DRC publicly questioned the long-term detention of political opponents of the government. Religious conflict in South Africa is increasingly rife within once relatively unified churches.

International opinion, which started turning against the country at the time of the Sharpeville shootings, has solidified into intense disapproval leading to extensive economic sanctions and disinvestment policies during the past few years. Since I focus more particularly on the handling of this particular form of South African conflict rather than on its actual manifestation, this topic will be discussed in Chapter 5.

Conclusion

One major feature of the protest movement is the durability and resilience of black resistance. Blacks have taken the initiative and white politics are largely formulated in response to black protest. The 1973 Durban strikes and the Soweto uprising in 1976 marked a resurgence of protest and increased mobilization, especially among blacks. As Stadler has pointed out in a recent publication:

> Despite the massive scale of the state repression which they provoked, oppositional activities generated and maintained a momentum entirely

at variance with the pattern exhibited during earlier periods of intense conflict. After the massacre at Sharpeville, and the banning of the African National Congress in 1960, a depression lasting for more than a decade settled over African politics.

But since the mid-1970s, the period of recuperation required before people returned to political struggles shortened. Formerly, repression exercised against one target had a deadening effect on other groups and organisations. In recent times, one form of resistance has fed into another.

(Stadler 1987: 1-2)

Tom Lodge also comments on this phenomenon:

The resistance of the 1970s provides a startling contrast in terms of scale and duration to the movements of the 1950s and early 1960s. This has reflected a fundamental crisis in South African society, in its origins both economic and political, a crisis which the authorities are apparently incapable of resolving through reform.

(Lodge 1983: 321)

This upsurge of black protest and its spirit of assertiveness are related to the development of trade union politics, the growth of militant community-based politics, the spread of the ideology of Black Consciousness, and changing structural conditions. This growing assertiveness can be seen as

. . . one of the corollaries of economic expansion . . . the growth of an African clerical workforce. Primary and secondary education had contributed to a sharply rising growth in the number of people who were literate; this was reflected in the development of a tabloid mass circulation press — Johannesburg's black population by 1970 was supporting two daily newspapers.

(Lodge 1983: 324)

The growing protest of the working masses was now receiving support from the black petty bourgeoisie, a relatively conservative sector which the government was attempting to co-opt, but which was becoming deeply alienated and frustrated (Nolutshungu 1983: 119-20). In addition to political restrictions on upward mobility, economic recession and unemployment were blocking progress.

Regional developments in Southern Africa strengthened protest even further. The southward sweep of the tide of revolution did much to heighten township optimism and generated the feeling that the days of the South African régime were numbered. What has also become clear in surveying the full range of manifestations of conflict is that, while white–black conflict is continuing, there are now other sources of conflict that increasingly cut across racial divides. There are whites and blacks on both sides of most conflicts. These new divisions and new alliances can be interpreted in terms of new sources of conflict — the subject of Chapter 4.

Chapter four

Shifting Bases of Conflict, Divisions, and Alliances

The preoccupation with the policy of apartheid on both sides of the divide has tended to obscure objective analyses and understanding of the major issues underlying the conflict in South Africa. Because conflict in South Africa has been conceptualized primarily in terms of race, we may ourselves tend to fall into the trap of seeing race as the root cause of that conflict. The danger of such an oversimplification is that one would then seek a remedy in terms of one narrow solution (i.e. the elimination of racial discrimination).

While race is a major source and dimension of conflict, the entire phenomenon of conflict is far more complex. For analytical purposes I have distinguished between three major dimensions of the social structure: economic, political, and socio-cultural. Because of the subjective bases of conflict, various aspects of these dimensions acquire comparatively more or less importance for action at certain times.

In Chapter 2 I argued that conflict in South Africa is multi-dimensional, and in Chapter 3 I reviewed ten different types of manifestations of conflict and violence. In the present chapter I look at the changing character of conflict in South Africa. I analyze the major ideological underpinnings of traditional apartheid and describe a shift in the prevailing white ideology. This shift represents a move away from socio-cultural thinking and towards economic perceptions of the social structure; from an ideology of racial and cultural priority to more practical, economic considerations. While I interpret this as a shift from ideological to more pragmatic considerations, it appears that the economy, like race, soon becomes the object of ideological interpretation. Ideological divisions then cut across divisions between rich and poor, white and black.

The role of ideology in conflict

Although material resources play an important role they are not the only factors that generate conflict. In all communities ideologies exist that cut across the structural features of society. These ideologies may be concerned with issues such as race or class and may be shared by members of varying racial groups and social classes. (For an excellent and detailed discussion of the role of ideologies in South Africa, see *Contending Ideologies in South Africa*, edited by James Leatt, Theo Kneifel, and Klaus Nürnberger, published by David Philip in 1986.)

When ideological commitment transcends the structural conditions of race or class membership, the basic conflict will be between the protagonists of the opposing ideologies and not between the races or the classes. Goals, interests, and values can acquire ideological meaning that will motivate people to act independently of their objective structural conditions of existence.

Some ideologies are defensive, serving mainly to rationalize or justify a satisfying order. For example, ideologies of management have sought to justify the subordination of large masses of men to the discipline of factory work and to the authority of employers. Other ideologies, such as socialism, are critical of the *status quo* in most western societies and are orientated towards the future. They attempt to formulate alternative perspectives for group life.

Mannheim distinguished two types of ideology: those which directed activities towards the maintenance of the existing order and those which generated activities leading towards changes in the prevailing order. Ideological motivation accounts for the 'defection' from their own group by whites who support the cause of blacks in South Africa, and by bourgeois intellectuals who support and promote the interests of the working class.

> Because of their identification with this ideology, liberal and socialist parties have been able to attract considerable support which they could not otherwise have won. Many individuals whose economic interest would normally lead them to support conservative parties have been won over by ideological appeals. This has been especially true of intellectuals, who are, by the virtue of their vocation, vulnerable to such appeals.
>
> (Lenski 1966: 419)

Ideology also accounts for the way in which, in every nation where free elections are held, large numbers of working-class members support conservative parties. In Britain, for example, the Conservative Party has enjoyed the support of a quarter to a third of the members of the working class. In the United States the Republican Party has been supported by half of the working class in presidential elections.

While clashes between broadly different social ideologies can be the cause of severe conflict in the wider social context, conflict over norms and methods between adherents of the same ideology can be just as intense. Extremely vehement disagreement often arises between different factions of liberation groups. Developments in the Palestine Liberation Organization provide a good example.

The ideology of apartheid

The extent to which ideology and indoctrination play a predominant role in South Africa was pointed out in two books by a prominent Afrikaner academic, Nic Rhoodie, who wrote in the late 1950s that 'the Afrikaner people, as a whole, believe firmly in the ideal of comparatively complete geo-physical separation (of the races)' (Rhoodie and Venter 1960: 31). The authors surmised that 'at least 80 per cent of the whites (in South Africa) are adherents to the basic principles of separate development . . .' (1960: 28). A decade later Rhoodie described white ideological commitment in even stronger terms:

> One reason why it is relatively easy for the present day researcher to compound a comprehensive image of apartheid policy is that it is . . . a comprehensive and complete system of ethnic relations founded on clearly formulated principles ideologically rooted in an unmistakable philosophy of life and . . . geared to the realisation of an ethnic system which, in all essential respects, is already subscribed to by the mass of right-wing whites as a practically attainable ideal.
> (Rhoodie 1969: 78)

Under Verwoerd's stewardship, apartheid rapidly developed into an ideology. Apartheid was not, according to Verwoerd, 'merely a collection of loosely formed ideas, nor does it merely touch here and there on some or other point, but is a programme that reaches out to affect the life circumstances of people in order to make them happy, to help avoid clashes, and to bring peace and order' (cited in Rhoodie 1969: 78). The South African policy of apartheid has to a remarkable degree succeeded in ordering itself into an articulated ideology founded on a value system and an outlook on life which has stretched back over more than 300 years (1969: 78).

With the development of apartheid ideology in the 1940s and 1950s, Afrikaner politics was slowly but fatally being theologized. 'It is not wholly correct to say that the DRC was or became the National Party at prayer, it is more correct to say that the National Party was itself becoming, if not a Church, then a party imbued with religion — a secular religion — at its very root', wrote W.A. de Klerk (1975: 199). 'This was nationalism as a world view, which did not accommodate itself to the human being who has acquired it, but which directed and led such a human being and made a servant of him' (1975: 205). According to the Afrikaner's own view of Christian Nationalism, blacks would develop their own culture and spiritual aristocracy. This too, according to De Klerk, would be 'Christian Nationalism' by nature. Thus there developed a close connection between nationhood, 'self-determination', and the homeland policy of separate development which was based on the specifically South African interpretation of neo-Calvinist teachings.

Despite the determination and commitment of nationalist leadership, as well as comprehensive propaganda and widespread indoctrination, apartheid both as a policy and a formal ideology has, since the mid-1970s, faced an increasingly severe crisis. This can be ascribed to various causes. First, it gradually became apparent that the Bantustan policy had failed in almost every respect. Second, over the previous two decades the 'moral' base of apartheid became eroded in Afrikaner circles. And third, the official Dutch Reformed Church doctrine of biblical support for apartheid crumbled in the early 1980s after having resisted for decades the onslaughts of English-language churches, of the World Council of Churches, and of its own dissidents.

While neo-Calvinist ideology has remained a force to be reckoned with among some Afrikaner leadership groups, the major proponents of the Verwoerdian ideology in cultural religious and political circles have been peripheralized in current top nationalist circles and many major governmental institutions have come to be dominated by pragmatists. The 1983 campaign for the referendum on the new constitutional proposals brought into the open the deep and intense schism between conservative Afrikaners who adhere dogmatically to the neo-Calvinist interpretations of the Bible, on which Verwoerd founded his vision of a white Utopia, and those who are abandoning this ideology. This schism manifested itself in the formation of the Conservative Party in 1983, led by the former DRC-minister, DR A.P. Treurnicht, a well-known proponent of the Calvinist doctrine.

Erosion of the moral base of apartheid

There has been a gradual extension into South Africa of the growing international consensus about the immorality of discrimination linked to racial, ethnic, or religious differences. The world has accepted the premiss that human beings do not have the right to exploit each other. Contemporary values make it difficult to justify the inequality of reward that exists in South Africa.

Well over a century ago de Tocqueville wrote that once the idea of equality entered the world it would be impossible to resist it and the forces advocating equality would eventually prevail. This is indeed happening in South Africa. Within this perspective, S.M. Lipset wrote:

Yet the rulers of white South Africa like the rulers of Communist Russia cannot maintain their unity against the underprivileged, for their need to have universities, to have intellectuals, scientists, educated professionals, forces them to create growing strata of intellectuals and students whose values and principles lead them to break up the united front of the governing White elite. The university world, all over the world, believes in universalistic and egalitarian values, and requires freedom in order to exist. Hence, it is inherently pitted against racism and authoritarianism. And just as universities in Russia, in Hungary, in Poland, in Spain, and in Greece, have erected fortresses from which men fight for freedom, so also in South Africa they must become growing centres of unrest within the system of racial domination. The sense that the racial distribution of power and privilege is morally wrong will penetrate into other segments of the country's elite from the universities. The questioning of the propriety of the system will not overturn it, will not make many white South Africans give up their privileges through emigration or other activities, but it will undermine their capacity to act ruthlessly against their own children demonstrating for equality, and even against the black Africans. For once men accept the fact that unequal treatment is immoral, they cannot use the kind of force which is necessary to maintain it. The conscience of the world has expressed that judgement on South African institutions. And unless South Africa closes down its universities, those universities must help train generations of young people who will see that their elders, their society, simply do not live up to the standards they proclaim, whether the ideal be separate but equal or equal and integrated.

The moral problems which concern South African students and intellectuals . . . have no resolution other than a radical change in the major social institutions of the country.

(S.M. Lipset in van der Merwe and Welsh 1972: 6–7)

One aspect of the erosion of discrimination was the changing perception of the concept of race. The belief that race determines one's physical, mental, and even moral qualities was generally accepted until a few decades ago. This view formed the basis of racial discrimination during the colonial period, and was justified by the presumed inherent or inborn differences between races. South Africa was slower than most Western countries to reject this theory and although intellectuals and liberal political leaders in South Africa have campaigned for many years for a new interpretation of 'race', nationalist politicians only recently started taking a public stand against racial discrimination.

The new interpretation of the concept 'race' has brought about a new look at the policy of racial discrimination. While the right-wing parties still believe in the inherent inequality of races and for that reason propagate racial discrimination, this approach is being publicly denounced today in government circles.

Theological retraction

For many years the official DRC stand on racial politics received wide public support from the members of the Reformed Church family: the Nederduits Gereformeerde Kerk, the Hervormde Kerk and the Gereformeerde Kerk. Their pro-apartheid stand was strongly criticized by the English-language churches and political opponents. Dissenters within these churches were severely reprimanded by high-handed and ruthless authoritarian church leaders such as Dr Koot Vorster. Some, like Dr Beyers Naude, were ostracized, others like Dr W.A. Landman, were silenced, and the lesser voices were merely ignored, or ridiculed and forgotten.

But in spite of a rigid, authoritarian atmosphere in the DRC the consciences of Nationalist Afrikaners were constantly being aroused, especially by cautious theologians of the Gereformeerde Kerk, who expressed loyal criticism from within the group. As the church gradually freed itself from the autocratic control of its conservative hierarchy, renewal became possible. The major impetus for this renewal came from the 'sister' churches, more specifically the N.G. Sendingkerk (Mission Church) under the influence of the dynamic theologian Dr Allan Boesak, who succeeded in getting his church to declare apartheid as a heresy.

In due course the Western Cape Synod of the DRC in 1983 and eventually the General Synod in 1986 made historic policy changes, stating that apartheid could not be scripturally justified. In so doing the DRC at last accepted the position which they had rejected under pressure from Verwoerd during the Cottesloe debate of 1960. The conflict between the Afrikaner's religious and political principles, predicted as far back as 1954 by the conservative historian G.D. Scholtz, had now developed. The theological base of apartheid was crumbling. Adherence to religious principles could no longer be reconciled with the practice of apartheid.

This reinterpretation of biblical truths by the DRC's sister churches and its Western Cape and General Synods was by no means shared by all their members, or by the other regional synods. It was inevitable that the bitter political division which developed among Afrikaners around the new constitutional proposals and led to the formation of the Conservative Party, would also lead to formal organizational rearrangements among the Reformed churches and the eventual establishment of the conservative Afrikaanse Protestantse Kerk (APK).

While the decline of apartheid ideology can be attributed in large part to the erosion of its moral and theological bases, this development should not necessarily be seen as a growth of altruism amongst whites. Self-interest and the wish to retain political and economic power remain major motivating forces. *Verligte* politicians have come to believe, or so they proclaim, that racial discrimination and a free market economy are incompatible.

But the decline of apartheid ideology does not necessarily spell the end of discrimination in South Africa. It merely means that it is practised in a new and different way. To understand this it is necessary to look at the significance of the difference between pragmatic and ideological politics.

Where racial discrimination is practised for ideological reasons, its ultimate aim is racial purity. Conflict is conceptualized as conflict with other racial groups. The Conservative Party (CP) and Herstigte Nasionale Party (HNP), for example, still see the South African struggle as one essentially between whites and non-whites. While this group is not currently in power, it is not inconceivable that they may gain power in the white Parliament in due course or that this conservative racist element may resurface in the National Party itself.

When politics is guided by pragmatic considerations, however, discrimination is no longer seen as an end in itself. It is a means by which economic and political goals can be achieved. Apartheid policy is now being assessed in pragmatic, instrumental terms: the question is — will it deliver the goods?

This pragmatic approach has enabled the current leadership to question the function and use of apartheid in a way that was not possible in the Verwoerdian era of Afrikaner thinking. Apartheid and racial discrimination have become 'negotiable'. In such a situation the dividing lines need not necessarily be racial ones, as they were traditionally conceived. Discrimination against *some* black groups may be more efficacious than against all. The National Party's pragmatic wing believes that if whites hope to retain a share in political and economic control in the long run, they will have to share power with other population groups. In the new dispensation of the tri-cameral parliament, racial discrimination is relaxed sufficiently to encourage a large number of coloured people and Indian leaders to attempt to make the new scheme work.

Indeed, this is precisely the charge that has been made against the government by South African socialists and Marxists. They argue that the government is attempting to co-opt an emerging 'black middle class' by giving them special (albeit still limited) rights which are withheld from the majority.

New interest groups are being created which cut across the black–white divide. New alliances are developing. But so, of course, are new divisions. Blacks, as well as whites, are divided. This was well illustrated in the review of manifestations of conflict in the previous chapter.

Reformulation of interests: market vs. controlled economy

The changes within Nationalist ideology have to be understood in relation to changes in the objective conditions of economic development, which have resulted in dramatic and fundamental changes in the structural conditions of white rule. The very arena of struggle, the terrain on which conflict occurs, has been transformed. These changes have not only made possible the existence of an increasingly militant black working class and a vocal, politically-conscious and disaffected black petty bourgeoisie — they have also transformed the nature of the ruling group itself.

Marxist scholarship brought new insights into the relationship between contending groups and forces in South Africa. Liberal historians and economists, accepting a liberal *laissez-faire* capitalist economic policy, have argued that this economic policy is irreconcilable with the practice of racial discrimination. Marxist scholars disagree. They have demonstrated the manner in which, under South African conditions, racial discrimination and capitalist exploitation have come to feed on and reinforce one another. Although the migrant labour system and the homeland policy placed constraints upon economic development, they provided the privileged sector of the economy with exactly what it needed: a large pool of readily available black migrant workers at low wages. As Dan O'Meara points out:

> Apartheid was much more than a tool to advance the interests of NP supporters. More fundamentally, it secured the interests of the entire capitalist class, enabling all capitalists to intensify the exploitation of African workers and so to raise the general rate of profit . . .
>
> Far from representing the triumph of the pre-capitalist frontier which undermined capitalism, as the conventional wisdom has it, the apartheid policies of the NP were a product of the particular character of capitalist development in South Africa and acted as a spur to rapid capital accumulation in a given historical phase of South African capitalism.
>
> (O'Meara 1983: 247)

However, with the development of the manufacturing industry in South Africa, which required skilled workers, the migrant system and influx control became untenable. In addition, the manufacturing industry was dependent on an expanding market. Ill-paid migrant workers were poor consumers. Increased buying power of the African population promised an expanding market. It became apparent that Verwoerdian apartheid could not be maintained in the expanding economy. Market principles had to replace racial criteria in determining access to opportunities within the capitalist social structure (Stadler 1987: 2).

The growing emphasis on the pursuit of profit in the capitalist system resulted in fundamental divisions within the Afrikaner community. This new direction taken by the National Party deprived it of its populist base — it became a party of the bourgeoisie. The basis of Afrikaner nationalist ideology was transformed from traditional apartheid to the promotion of a market economy. English capital, the traditional exploiter, became a partner in the pursuit of profit.

The rearrangement of priorities in the National Party has paved the way for considerations other than racial purity to provide the major unifying and motivating forces of the emerging mixed establishment and, similarly, of the emerging mixed opposition. However, the waning of the apartheid ideology, more pragmatic approaches to the regulation of race relations, and greater emphasis on socio-economic matters do not necessarily mean that the conflict will become confined to mere structural issues and competition for scarce resources. Ideologies fulfil basic human needs and the development of conflicting ideologies around perceptions and models of the socio-economic system is inevitable.

While there is no clearly formulated ideology on either side of the new political divide in South Africa there are indications that conflicting themes are emerging on opposite sides. Race, obviously, will remain an important distinguishing factor between the major opposing groups in South Africa while power is still largely concentrated in white hands. But the establishment is gradually acquiring certain conspicuous features and espousing certain values which will largely determine the basis on which new alignments and coalitions can be formed, many of them across the colour line.

Sam Nolutshungu (1983: 2, 17, 109) gives a perceptive picture of what he calls 'the reformist position in the emerging establishment'. While the various groups do not contain a central theory, they share certain themes:

- liberal notions of society and social change;
- a general commitment to preserve the basic capitalist order, with private though hardly free enterprise;
- an antipathy to revolution; and
- a continued process of de-racialization leading to the outward forms of multi-racial rule.

Slabbert and Welsh (1979: 6) argue that this kind of rigidly controlled change, which they describe as siege under a modernizing oligarchy, will lead to increasing ideological polarisation: 'Ideological polarization means that the economic system will be increasingly questioned and attacked by blacks and defended by whites.' Particularly the younger generation of blacks is beginning to question the validity of the free enterprise economic system.

Their demands are no longer directed to inclusion within an economic and political structure but to the substitution of an entirely different one. To the extent that racial and ideological polarisation coincide, i.e. that race and class become synonymous in the minds of the majority of particularly the urban blacks, to that extent the conflict situation becomes less negotiable in South Africa.

(Slabbert and Welsh 1979: 6)

The conflict in the economic sphere is moving from the structural level (claims to scarce resources) to the level of values and ideologies. Fanatical commitment to these ideologies may reduce the chances of a negotiated settlement. The espousal of the free enterprise system has become a distinguishing feature of a wide range of interest groups that constitute what we regard as the emerging establishment. The rejection of capitalism and the espousal of some form of socialism, often referred to as African socialism, has characterized a wide range of groups that we define as the opposition operating outside the existing socio-economic system in South Africa.

While the South African economy could be defined as a market-oriented, free enterprise or capitalist system, it obviously falls far short of the true model. Variations of capitalism and socialism have become the major 'conservative' and 'radical' rallying points of the emerging establishment and opposition respectively.

Free enterprise, rather than racial purity or superiority, is now the major slogan of the government. The government-controlled SABC argues that South Africa looks to free enterprise as an indispensable agent in shaping its new economic and social destiny. An editorial comment stated:

Free enterprise stands at the very centre of the conflict of ideas — economic, political and religious — which is joined around the world as the 20th Century draws to a close. Opposed to it is socialism.
(South African Broadcasting Corporation, Comment 2.7.82)

Ardent proponents from the business section who are critical of the apartheid policy argue that free enterprise actually helps to promote greater justice and equality, countering the discriminatory forces of apartheid.

In an editorial in *Die Burger* (18 August 1982), the senior pro-government paper, it is argued that the National Party (a) has committed itself to the removal of 'unjust discriminatory practices and regulations' and (b) supports a free market economy. The editorial supports Prof Jan Lombard who believes that the removal of discriminatory legislation which impedes free economic development, would lead to the narrowing of the wage gap. The editorial concludes that social justice can be achieved more readily by a free economy than by political measures: 'after a thorough investigation, as proposed by Prof Lombard, it will appear that it is much easier to achieve greater social justice by means of economic measures than through political action'.

In an editorial comment on 20 October 1982 the SABC stated that many 'articulate' men in America and Europe believe that

> free enterprise is superior to socialism both economically and morally. They do not deny that the true capitalist is motivated by self-interest but they refute the charge that it is a narrow self-interest: it is as wide as the markets he hopes to supply, as extended as the needs of his fellow men that he proposes to satisfy. By comparison, socialism is sterile. It stifles individual initiative which is at the heart of the free human spirit.

Conservatives argue that those developing countries which have followed the free enterprise system have demonstrably out-performed those which, at an early stage in their development, have favoured some form of socialism. They argue that the performance of predominantly free enterprise countries, such as Taiwan, Kenya, Brazil and South Korea, is much better than those which have favoured some variant of socialism such as Cuba, Tanzania, Zambia, and Ghana.

The increasingly ardent and vocal commitment to the free enterprise system has made big business a natural ally of the *verligte* Nationalist government. While the nature and extent of collaboration between government and big business (apartheid and capital) in the past is a matter of great dispute in academic and political circles, there is an open and growing alliance between the pragmatists in the new regime and leaders of industry and commerce. The Carlton and Good Hope discussions and anti-inflation consultations of the 1980s are conspicuous manifestations of this symbiosis. This relationship was given a big boost by the sweeping policy announcements by the State President at the opening of the 1988 Parliament and by subsequent steps towards privatization of the economy.

The emerging free market ideology provides the basis for the co-option or integration of black interest groups into the establishment.

As the ideology of free enterprise was taking shape in the white establishment and among those interest groups that increasingly tended to line up with the government, so the ideology of 'socialism' was, inevitably, taking shape as the dominant ideology of opposition groups, albeit in many forms. Some opposition groups are merely sympathetic to socialism while others are committed to it.

Ideological commitment of a Marxist or socialist brand can be as fierce as or fiercer than commitment to apartheid or Nazism because there are similar convictions of moral superiority or divine election.

Intense anti-capitalist sentiment and commitment to a socialist system as the solution for South Africa was forcefully formulated by a South African exile and prominent anti-apartheid leader in England, Cosmas Desmond. In his book, aptly titled *Christians or Capitalists*, he writes: 'I am a Christian and because I am a Christian I am a socialist.' This commitment 'is the result of my experience in South Africa' (Desmond 1978: 10). Quoting Karl Barth, he argues that God always takes his stand 'against the lofty and on behalf of the lowly'. 'If we are to take the same ideological stand we obviously cannot assume a capitalist stance' (1978: 77). The church is guilty of an unquestioning acceptance of the capitalist model of society. Desmond sees the evils of society as not simply caused by 'politics', but by a specific form of politics, namely capitalist politics. This, in his view, can only be overcome by socialist politics, which then becomes obligatory for Christians.

Capitalism is regarded as synonymous with the accumulation of wealth and this is clearly contrary to Christ's injunction not to 'store up treasures on earth'. Capitalist values are diametrically opposed to New Testament norms and as such are immoral (Desmond 1978: 111-18). Desmond accepts that not all blacks will be converted to this ideology. In the Marxist tradition of attributing this failure to false consciousness, he argues: 'Some Black Christians, because of their indoctrination in a different understanding of Christianity, might not accept it in theoretical terms' (1978: 24).

This developing ideological polarization in South Africa is seen by many as a microcosm of world conflict. John Killick (1983: 5), former British Ambassador to the USSR, sees it in a rather sinister way:

> So Southern Africa, and South Africa par excellence, must be regarded as a glittering prize in the continuing struggle between socialism and capitalism — perhaps decisive in its importance as a source of gold, diamonds and industrial minerals, not to mention its strategic position astride major sea routes.

The movement away from racial discrimination and towards greater adherence to the principles of the free market will inevitably lead to stronger ties between the present South African establishment and conservative free market oriented governments, such as those of Reagan and Thatcher.

The success of the American policy of constructive engagement can be measured in terms of the extent to which there was movement away from racial discrimination and movement towards a free market. This is in large measure related to the extent that South Africa is seen as a microcosm of the world conflict between capitalism, as espoused by the Reagan administration, and international socialism or communism.

Political divisions and alliances in flux

The politics of pragmatism have had the effect of redefining the battle lines in the South African political struggle. The essential values and motivating forces that are holding together the major political configurations are changing and the change process is leading to new alignments. The changing priorities of the National Party are providing new rallying forces in the emerging mixed establishment. As the nature of the establishment changes, the nature of the traditional opposition groups is changing too, and new opposition groups are emerging. Opposition groups that used to rally automatically around anti-apartheid issues are increasingly basing their policies more on socio-economic issues. They are also tending to challenge the legitimacy of the very system within which parliamentary (and most legal) politics are conducted. Because the current socio-economic system has been and continues to be accepted relatively uncritically by both establishment and current parliamentary opposition, the opposition within parliament has become less relevant and often tends to merge with the establishment in defence against the onslaught upon the socio-economic system.

This state of flux in South African politics can best be understood by distinguishing between three major alliances or configurations of interest groups (van der Merwe 1981: 19; van der Merwe 1982: 330–1; van der Merwe 1983b; Hund and van der Merwe 1986, chapter 4; Webb and van der Merwe 1987).

The establishment alliance. Race will always be a divisive factor in South Africa but whereas the establishment used to be exclusively white and motivated by the traditional wish to maintain white purity, this is much less so today. It is now more motivated by a business ideology, that of a free market, and efficiency. On this basis, coalitions can be established across the colour barrier. The establishment is gradually incorporating blacks that share these values and is increasingly catering for the interests of blacks who have a commitment to, and vested interest in, the protection of the prevailing socio-economic system.

The establishment alliance includes the National Party and to an increasing extent the coloured and Indian parties participating in the new constitutional dispensation. (For detailed discussions of the positions of political parties and groups, see *South Africa: No easy path to peace* by Graham Leach, published by Routledge in 1986.) In a peripheral sense it also includes African bodies such as Community Councils operating under government auspices.

The alliance of opposition groups within the socio-economic system (*i.e. intra-systemic opposition*), including parliamentary and extraparliamentary groups. This alliance includes parliamentary opposition and other groups such as business sectors and trade unions which have opposed the government on race issues but are willing to co-operate *within the broad socio-economic system of a market-oriented economy*. As state policy shifts and the government removes race discrimination, and takes a more consistent stand in favour of free enterprise, this group finds itself increasingly in sympathy with the party in power.

The intra-systemic opposition groups want political change, but at the same time they seek to avoid any dislocation of productivity, and want to maintain the nature of the economic system. To an extent this alliance includes the Progressive Federal Party (PFP), big business, and the coloured and Indian parties, and African councils mentioned above. It also includes the KwaZulu Legislative Assembly, Inkatha and the United Workers Union of South Africa (UWUSA). Seen from within the current political system, they constitute the opposition to the ruling National Party. But seen in the light of the capitalist-socialist struggle in South Africa, they are becoming part of the establishment.

The current failure of the Nationalist Government to come to terms with the leaders of Inkatha and of the KwaNatal Indaba should not distract observers from the obvious potential for co-operation between establishment leaders and Inkatha leaders. Inkatha has consistently taken a firm stand in favour of a market economy and a pragmatic approach, and is willing to compromise in order to accommodate white needs in a multiracial government (De Kock 1986: 114). The success of the Indaba between the KwaZulu government and the Natal Provincial Administration is a hopeful example of inter-racial co-operation between white and black and between parliamentary and extra-parliamentary parties.

The alliance of opposition groups operating outside the current socioeconomic and political framework (i.e. *the extra-systemic opposition*). These groups fall outside the framework in two respects: (a) They are excluded from and/or refuse to participate in the current political structures created by the Government, such as Parliament, the President's Council, Community Councils, and homeland governments; (b) They reject the predominantly capitalist socio-economic system and favour a socialized and controlled economy, industrial democracy, or related systems.

This category includes organizations such as the United Democratic Front (UDF), the Congress of South African Trade Unions (Cosatu), the National Forum, the Azanian Peoples' Organization (Azapo), the Pan Africanist Congress (PAC), and the African National Congress (ANC). They see the basic issues not so much in racial but in socio-economic terms. They seek fundamental change in the socio-economic system along broadly socialist lines. They regard the PFP, Inkatha and similar organizations as part of the capitalist establishment. This third group has emerged as a major political movement in South Africa, opposing the emerging re-grouped 'establishment' described above.

To sum up, the major emerging political division is not between whites and blacks but between those who adhere to or propagate the free enterprise ideology and the proponents of a broadly socialist or hard-line Marxist approach. The extent to which future policies, practices and strategies will conform to these ideologies, however, will remain to be seen. The Government, while claiming to be a major proponent of free enterprise, is often accused of merely paying lip-service to this system. The ANC, on the other hand, while being 'formally committed to socialism', is 'hardly doctrinaire' about it (Lodge 1983: 84).

The Freedom Charter, the manifesto of the ANC and of the UDF, calls for a socialization and a radical redistribution of wealth but these goals could be met by a system of social democracy in which state-controlled organizations coexist with private enterprise (Hund 1988: 217–28). Lodge (1983: 84) maintains that

> The main source of radical pressure or influence on the ANC leadership does not come either from its eastern bloc allies or, as is often asserted, from its members who are also communist. With the renaissance of popular political culture during the post-Soweto era there has developed a profound and widespread antipathy to capitalism.

In conflict situations the espousal of a certain ideology by one side is often based primarily on the aversion for or total rejection of the ideology of the opponent and is thus more of a negative counter-ideology than a positive commitment.

The emerging fundamental divide in our society is no more between white and black, between government and parliamentary opposition. Neither is it between parliamentary and extra-parliamentary groups. It is, of course, true that there are serious divisions between these groups that have been traditional opponents. Inkatha, the major extra-parliamentary intra-systemic opposition group feel they are making no progress in their relations with the government. But in a more fundamental way in the long term the division between Inkatha and the UDF resembles a greater political divide than between Inkatha and the government.

In our search for the constructive accommodation of conflict in South Africa, our primary task should be to assess the prospects of communication, dialogue, negotiation, and comparatively peaceful settlement of differences between the two major emerging groups: the expanding establishment and the extra-systemic opposition operating outside the prevailing socio-economic system.

In this chapter I have focused on the major ideologies and goals that distinguish the emerging establishment. In Chapter 5 I will discuss their disagreements as to means. The intra-systemic opposition tends to accept incremental steps while the extra-systemic opposition tends to demand radical change as a condition for participation and co-operation.

Chapter five

Approaches to Handling Conflict

As the spiral of violence increases and polarization intensifies, South Africa appears to many observers and protagonists to present a classic case of irreconcilable differences leading inevitably to cataclysmic confrontation. In this climate, words like negotiation, mediation and conciliation are treated in many circles as dirty words or, at best, irrelevant and inappropriate. Yet, in spite of numerous and formidable obstacles, there remain valid grounds for positive and constructive attitudes towards prospects for the eventual negotiated settlement in South Africa.

I have argued that conflict is endemic in society and can, indeed, serve useful functions. Unless handled constructively, however, it may lead to a vicious spiral of violence. Violence and non-violence have become topics of heated debate in South Africa. While usually abhorred in public rhetoric, especially by the establishment, violence is almost universally felt to be justified when committed by those with whom we sympathize.

Christian churches generally accept the 'just war' doctrine: the justification of violence as a last resort against aggression or tyranny. Few religious leaders adopt a pacifist stance and political leaders on either side of the conflict also justify using violence, under certain conditions, as a necessary means to obtain desirable ends.

Believing that violence is wasteful and destructive but nevertheless endemic in society, I argue that violence, as coercion, is best interpreted as a way of communicating with the adversary. Approached from this point of view, violence can be seen as complementary to negotiation, the more constructive form of communication.

Mismanagement of conflict and negative, destructive measures to accommodate conflict, are found in all parties in South Africa. In this chapter I discuss general and specific factors requiring clarification, and focus on some that exacerbate conflict and raise obstacles to rational negotiated settlement.

Pessimistic vs. Utopian schools

Current research on resolution of conflict is characterized by a relatively positive approach based on the belief that the resolution or, at least, constructive accommodation of conflict is more likely than has been traditionally assumed. The traditional negative or pessimistic approach stemmed largely from recognition of natural human aggression and the scarcity of finite material resources such as possessions and territory. Competition for resources was believed to rule out real resolution of conflict.

This pessimistic school of thought is largely based on two fundamental assumptions. The first is that the drive to dominate is universal in mankind. This belief is based on the views of Hobbes and Machiavelli and has been reinforced by Calvinist theology. Life is an eternal struggle between those on top and those struggling to get to the top. We cannot have peace, but we can have order — as long as those on top manipulate through threats or use coercion to maintain their position and impose their order upon others.

The epitomizing slogan is: If you want peace, prepare for war. This approach is reflected in a statement by Robert S. McNamara, former US Secretary of Defence: 'Security depends upon assuming a worst possible case, and having the ability to cope with it.'

The second assumption is that conflict arises from incompatible interests built into structures. This interpretation has been reinforced by Marxist analysis. Not only do policies exploit but so do structures. This perception often leads to the conclusion that conflict must be sharpened to undermine and destroy the exploitative structures. Any other course would be playing the game of the ruling elite by making people 'happy slaves'.

Pessimism about the South African conflict can therefore be partly ascribed to widely-felt traditional pessimism about conflict in general. At the other extreme is the 'Utopian blueprint school' which envisages a warless future achieved by the adoption of legal or constitutional blueprints for general disarmament or world government. This approach 'requires a heroic faith in the politically naive slogan that "what is desirable is indeed possible"' (Falk and Kim 1980: 4).

Constructive approaches to conflict

The belief that conflict *per se* is undesirable, and that the task of intervention or management is to eradicate conflict, is based on a fundamental misunderstanding of the role of conflict in society. It should rather be seen as one of society's 'engines of evolution', serving useful social functions and promoting growth and progress. The real problem does not lie in the presence of conflict but in the way it is handled, accommodated, or resolved. If handled negatively and destructively, conflict may end in violence — its extreme manifestation.

The most common ways of handling conflict are often the most inappropriate because they are based on gut feelings and emotion rather than on rational and cost-benefit analyses. Five conventional styles in handling conflict are usually distinguished:

Competing is assertive and uncooperative — a party pursues his own concerns at the other person's expense. This is a power-orientated mode using whatever power seems appropriate to win one's own position — one's ability to argue, one's rank, as well as economic sanctions. Competing might mean standing up for one's rights, defending a position which one believes is correct, or simply trying to win.

Smoothing is unassertive and co-operative — (often) tantamount to giving in. A 'smoothing' individual tries to preserve the relationship at all costs, emphasizing areas of agreement and failing to confront thorny issues.

Avoiding is unassertive and uncooperative — the party does not immediately pursue his own concerns or those of the other person. He does not address the conflict. Avoiding might take the form of diplomatically side-stepping an issue, postponing an issue until a better time, or simply withdrawing from a threatening situation.

Compromising is intermediate in both assertiveness and co-operativeness. The objective is to find some expedient, mutually acceptable solution which partially satisfies both parties. It falls on a middle ground between competing and accommodating. It addresses an issue more directly than avoiding, but does not explore the possibilities in as much depth as in joint problem-solving. Compromising might mean splitting the difference, exchanging concessions, or seeking a quick middle-ground position.

Joint problem-solving is both assertive and co-operative — the opposite of avoiding. Joint problem-solving involves working with the other party to find some solution which fully satisfies the concerns of both parties. It means digging into an issue to identify the underlying concerns of the two parties and to find an alternative which meets both sets of concerns. Joint problem-solving might take the form of exploring disagreement, to learn from each other's insights.

This approach provides the fairest alternative to violence in aggressively polarized societies or local communities. It is based on the following assumptions:

- That both parties are capable of competing but wish to avoid large-scale and violent confrontation.
- That there is sufficient common ground to make consultation worthwhile.

- That some mutually acceptable programme of change can be found through honest discussion.

Conflict is destructive when it diverts energy from important work or other issues, destroys morale, polarizes groups, deepens differences in values and produces violence. Conflict is constructive when it opens up and clarifies important issues and helps to solve them, increases involvement of individuals in important issues, makes communication more authentic, releases pent-up emotion, stress or anxiety, helps build group cohesiveness and helps individual growth, provided there is reflection on the conflict (Albert 1986: 4, 5). Conflict research should aim at enhancing creative and non-violent consequences of conflict and minimizing destructive consequences. The net reduction of human misery is the ultimate social objective of conflict analysis (Gurr 1980: 12).

The constructive approach to conflict accommodation is based on the belief that there are ways in which violence can be reduced. It is true that social structures tend to protect vested interests and that humans have a strong drive to dominate. But it is also true that the human species is infinitely creative and has devised and adapted many social structures in the service of more humane communities.

Conflict analysis includes, among other pursuits, developing and testing empirical theory about constructive handling of conflict. Social scientists have developed and promoted approaches and techniques that make resolution of conflict more likely than has previously been thought possible.

The following insights and principles underlie current constructive approaches to the accommodation of conflict, and they are certainly applicable in the South African situation.

1. While material resources may indeed be scarce and finite, a rational approach to their optimal development and exploitation may yield higher returns than those that could be gained by destructive competitive processes.
2. Non-material resources are not finite and need not be scarce. Resources such as skills, expertise and security have the tendency *to increase through use*. Sharing is, therefore, a way of increasing benefits.
3. Emphasis on the importance and satisfaction of needs, rather than on interests and values, is more likely to promote conflict resolution.
4. Perceptions, opinions, and attitudes are subjectively determined by the observer's social context. Clarification and recognition of these subjective observations will facilitate conflict resolution.
5. Prospects of improved meaningful communication between con-

flicting groups are a major source of a more positive and optimistic approach to conflict resolution.
6. Achievement of a number of win–win solutions has yielded encouraging results during the past decade or two, even in instances of serious conflict.

In this chapter I discuss various aspects of the South African situation and come to the conclusion that constructive accommodation of conflict in South Africa is becoming more likely in the light of these insights and approaches.

Negotiation and coercion

Constructive and destructive ways of communication between conflicting groups lie along a continuum of behaviour patterns. These patterns range between coercion (including violence) and co-operative behaviour (such as negotiation). Neither coercion nor negotiation constitutes distinct categories of behaviour and in practice distinctions between them often become blurred. While coercion (including violence) and co-operation (including negotiation) stand in a relationship of tension towards each other, they are not mutually exclusive. The presence of one does not rule out the other. This basic argument has important implications for interpreting behaviour by adversaries, by the public, and by the outside world.

Pressures are required to bring about change in South Africa. Negotiation should be seen as complementing pressure in the communication process between conflicting parties. By improving the quality of communication and understanding, negotiation will ensure more rational and effective pressures and more orderly change, so reducing the likelihood of destructive violence. Pressures on the South African government should be seen as part of the communication process, and should be constructive and conditional, rather than punitive. Thus the twin goals of justice and peace can be jointly served, rather than serving one at the expense of the other.

This approach cuts across the false but popular notion that negotiation and coercion are contradictory and mutually exclusive. To present to the public the impression that we have to choose between negotiation and coercion — the one leading to peace and justice and the other to domination and doom — is misleading. In fact, negotiation that lacks coercive power is unlikely to achieve any meaningful change in political relations. Coercion is part of the negotiation and bargaining process. The actual outcome is normally some kind of compromise between the two.

The case for negotiation for the High Road has been made persuasively by Clem Sunter in numerous presentations and in his well-documented book, *The World and South Africa in the 1990s* (1987). The High Road is the outcome of joint negotiation and synergy, 'whereby the final product is a great deal better than the separate parties to the process originally conceived'. The goal is a 'genuine democracy', where government is a 'servant of the people,' where power is decentralized because 'everybody is around the negotiating table' and all want a 'measure of regional and local autonomy'. He adds: 'There will be natural checks and balances' (1987: 105–6). This sounds like Utopia.

In the Low Road scenario a big and centralized government co-opts instead of negotiating with opposition groups. Conflicts and sanctions increase and the country becomes an isolated military fortress. The end game is the Waste Land (1987: 106). This is a prophecy of doom.

To visualize two alternatives is easy: we either negotiate and prosper, or coerce and be doomed. The danger is that we will envisage one scenario as entirely determined by negotiation and the other by full-scale coercion. Columnists have referred to the 'inescapable choice between a Low Road of authoritarian co-option and endemic violence and a High Road of genuine negotiations, stability and economic growth'. The real life scenario which I envisage is one in which interplay of negotiation and coercion — with doubtless some measure of excessive violence — will set us on a Middle Road. The Middle Road will be the grand realistic compromise.

Negotiation is an essential part of the democratic interaction of pressures in politics. It counteracts authoritarian polarization of politics which is exploited 'by both white ruler and black revolutionary to their own advantage' (Degenaar 1987: 6). We do not have a *choice* between negotiation and coercion. We must strive to achieve a *balance* between them. Neither the pessimistic nor the Utopian model is adequate. Imaginative pragmatism will find creative approaches to specific situations.

Coercion and co-operation are proper and useful modes of action in both domestic and international relations. Discussing relations between South Africa and her neighbours, John Barratt (1988: 3, 4) argues that 'neither conflict nor cooperation is a one-sided affair'. He writes:

> In spite of the conflictual relationships, plus the resentment of other states at the assertion of South African dominance, important functional links continue and in some cases are growing. Even more significant is that it is still possible, through patient negotiating processes and the preservation of channels of communication, to develop co-operative ventures where interdependence is a characteristic rather than a simple dependence. The attempts to restore the flow of electric power from Cahora Bassa and to develop the soda ash deposits

in Botswana, as well as the massive Highlands water scheme in Lesotho, are notable examples of a currently emerging pattern of cooperative ventures undertaken in spite of the continuing conflict.

These ventures developed because they meet the needs of participating countries. They demonstrate the paradox that incentives of mutual benefit can continue to operate while a conflictual relationship continues at another level. Centripetal and centrifugal forces operate at the same time.

Pressure provides impetus to change, to incorporate new lessons learned and to avoid stagnation. Co-operation generates a form of glue which strengthens the system, linking people and groups in common efforts. Parties use some combination of coercion and co-operation in attempting to achieve desired outcomes. Each also attempts to cause others to act in ways that will promote its interests. The means chosen depend largely on the analysis of the existing situation, what we might call the balance between justice and peace, as well as the balance of power.

Negotiation, communication, consultation, and co-option

Negotiation should always be seen within the broader context of the communication process between contending parties. This includes a range of modes of communication such as facilitation, mediation, and coercion.

Negotiation is a problem-solving process in which individuals or groups voluntarily discuss their differences and attempt to reach a joint decision about their mutual concerns. Negotiation is the principal way of mutually redefining an old relationship that is not operating satisfactorily or of establishing a new relationship where none existed before. The problem-solving approach seeks win–win solutions through negotiation in contrast to the traditional adversarial win–lose approach. But negotiation also includes a bargaining relationship in which coercion is used to influence the behaviour of the adversary. Bargaining refers to the process of making substantive, procedural, or psychological trade-offs to reach an acceptable settlement.

While communication is in its generic sense a 'neutral' word, it acquired a negative meaning among trade unions in the early 1970s when management used the word to describe a specific system of communication (liaison committees) manipulated by managers to control emerging unions. Communication was seen as a means to prevent negotiation. The word negotiation was not even mentioned in the original Black Labour Relations Regulation Act of 1953. Liaison committees were therefore channels whereby management communicated *to* rather than *with* workers. No wonder there was widespread rejection of these committees by the emerging trade unions.

Just as 'communication' has acquired a negative meaning in industrial relations, 'negotiation' has acquired a negative meaning in political relations. This has happened because the government has been using the term 'negotiation' to describe its strategies of consultation and co-option. Consultation implies no cost to the dominant party because it largely controls the process and sets the agenda. Furthermore, recent consultations have not been conducted with legitimate representatives of the black people, but with individuals, either appointed by the government or elected by processes which were not considered legitimate by the masses.

Social and psychological obstacles

I have already referred to the tendency to be pessimistic and negative about conflict. This tendency is exacerbated by a number of factors located in the social structure and in human nature.

Competitive processes are dominant in South African politics and tend to produce effects which perpetuate and escalate conflict. The view develops that the solution to any conflict has to be imposed by one side or the other by means of superior force, deception, or cleverness. This competitive hostility is reinforced by a perception of the scarcity of finite material resources, such as possessions and territory, and this is often seen as an insurmountable obstacle to conflict accommodation. The situation is perceived as a zero-sum game where they risk losing all.

There are, however, few circumstances so rigidly structured as to cause one's gains to come inevitably from the other's losses. To the extent that resources are logically and rationally developed and exploited, the contending parties may find a *modus operandi* based on a non-emotional cost analysis aimed at maximum gain for each party. This has become known as a win–win outcome in consensus politics.

Human aggressiveness and violence constitute major sources of conflict and obstacles to promoting peaceful relations. People tend to 'react' and behave in an emotional, irrational way. A high proportion of behaviour is unreasoned, unthinking, and highly subjective.

One reason for the perpetuation of apartheid is suggested by Festinger's theory of cognitive dissonance: that people tend to adjust their beliefs and attitudes to harmonize with their actions. Because apartheid has been imposed by law for the past forty years, pressure for self-consistency leads to a continuation of conflict. Past actions have to be justified to oneself and to others. The most direct reasons for South Africa's continued involvement in apartheid are the historical facts of our involvement in the past. It is exceedingly difficult to disengage and to acknowledge how purposeless and unthinking our past practices have been. Change is only possible through increasing awareness of longer or larger perspectives, encouraging consonance with constructive approaches.

Approaches to Handling Conflict

Conflict tends to be self-perpetuating. When it becomes institutionalized — part of certain institutions and structures — members of those institutions develop a vested interest in perpetuating that conflict. Decision makers are thus unable to terminate conflict even if they wish to do so. Conflict takes on an integrative function, often for both parties.

Senior members of military establishments are reluctant to see the end of war because this may end their careers. Protest and liberation movements within South Africa and abroad have also become 'institutionalized' in recent years and now offer career prospects. The anti-apartheid movement has in fact grown into a large industry in several countries, providing income, status and prestige, as well as a genuinely important cause, to large numbers of people. Its growth has been enhanced considerably by domestication and politicization of apartheid issues in overseas countries. Various interest groups have developed vested interests in the perpetuation of the apartheid issue.

In my mediation efforts on an international level my role as mediator has invariably been more warmly acknowledged by South African leaders of liberation movements in exile than by spokesmen of anti-apartheid and boycott movements of other nationalities. The latter seem to leave no room for a negotiated settlement. I have come to the reluctant conclusion that some of these advocates have a vested interest in perpetuating the conflict, while the South African leaders in exile are interested in exploring honourable settlements that would enable them to return home. On the other hand, leading members of the South African establishment believe that some ANC leaders are living so comfortably in exile that they do not wish to return to South Africa, where they would have to compete for jobs in a competitive society.

These exacerbating factors are further reinforced by unreliable and impoverished communication. This is especially true for relations between the establishment and opposition groups operating outside the system. They have to rely on espionage and other circuitous means of obtaining information. Errors and misinformation reinforce pre-existing attitudes and expectations.

While it is obvious that not all conflict can be reduced to mere misperception, parties to a conflict do have rigid ideas about the character and motives of their opponents, developed over years of biased information. Their selections from past history and their moral judgements justify, confirm, and reinforce their attitudes. Each party is predisposed to place the least favourable interpretation upon actions of the opposing side. Acts of horrific violence and brutal repression confirm each party's worst suspicions of the other and intensify moral outrage, fear, and retaliation.

Polarization erodes the middle ground and leads to rejection of moderates or peacemaking groups, such as white or black liberals, or 'moderates', 'verligtes' and 'pacifists'. Change-oriented groups do have reason to be sceptical of moderates advocating gradual change. Too often this is the tactic of those who want to retain vested interests. A situation then develops, however, in which all people who propagate reform rather than revolution, are automatically accused of wanting merely 'cosmetic change'. Pacifists are rejected on the grounds that they are merely passive. Non-violence is rejected as though it implies a failure to act at all.

Intense polarization makes it increasingly difficult for opponents to understand one another or even to communicate. Unless a middle ground can be occupied by a third party intervener to facilitate communication, opponents become increasingly entrenched in mutual distrust, fear and hostility.

Bargaining power, violence, and non-violence

A legitimate reason for scepticism about negotiation in South Africa is asymmetry of bargaining power between parties to conflict. Where great power disparity exists there is a danger that negotiation will be used by the more powerful party to co-opt or otherwise manipulate the weaker party, or to defuse the situation before the weaker party has mustered sufficient power or resources to seriously challenge the *status quo*.

Scarcely a day goes by that South African government-controlled media do not make reference to the desirability of negotiation as a means to resolve the national dilemma. Yet as long as negotiation is seen as likely to work to the advantage of the party with the most power, it will be regarded with suspicion by the weaker group, who fear that the process will be used to smooth over deep structural injustices in our society. Less powerful parties thus hesitate to call for mediation and negotiation, choosing rather to pursue goals such as social change and empowerment. Radical leaders prefer to channel the energies of the oppressed community into community building intended to increase their bargaining power.

An essential component in successful negotiation is balance of power: in a situation where both parties hold power, each party is able to exert pressures and inflict cost on the other. However, if one party is excessively weak and unable to impose substantial costs, it cannot have any meaningful impact on the opponent's behaviour or on the outcome of the process.

The ever-increasing spiral of violence and polarization is another reason for viewing the current South African situation as unfavourable to a negotiated settlement. Violence committed by both government and opposition, both physically and in the form of structural or institutional violence, poses a major stumbling block to negotiations.

While violence is usually abhorred in public rhetoric, all politicians and virtually the entire Christian church believe that violence in its most destructive form, warfare, can be justified under certain conditions. The theology of a just war dates back to the early history of almost all Christian churches. And its relevance to the current South African situation has been emphasized by the Kairos Theologians (1985) who stated: 'There is a long and consistent Christian tradition about the use of physical force to defend oneself against aggressors and tyrants. In other words, there are circumstances when physical force may be used.'

South African church leaders, including Nobel Peace laureate Desmond Tutu, do not opt for a pacifist stand and it is therefore most unlikely that any political leaders will support pacifism. Like religious leaders, they will not in principle renounce it. They will reserve the right to use violence as a last resort. If they are in power they will use it to maintain law and order to suppress protest, rebellion, armed revolution, or invasion by foreign powers. If they are in opposition and believe that all normal channels of protest have been closed and that the government is completely intransigent, they will inevitably resort to violence, believing that justice is on their side. Depending on the political and moral convictions of the clergy, they will rally behind either those in authority or those in rebellion, arguing that God is on their side.

The term violence has very broad implications and is by no means the exclusive province of disgruntled minorities or those out of power. Governments use violence consistently to achieve their goals, through psychological, institutional, and structural means (Kaunda 1980: 41, 127). Institutional violence, for example, involves the use of physical force by agents of the state, such as police and troops. Structural violence can be seen in the systematic denigration and deprivation of certain legally-defined population groups, by structures within the society.

Many regard intensification of the struggle in South Africa as an indication that negotiation is ruled out. Quite the contrary may be true. It is normal for parties in conflict to do their best to increase their bargaining power before negotiations commence. It is also normal for political leaders (both ANC and government) to publicly deny negotiations at such times.

I have argued that, in the pursuit of the goals of justice and peace in South Africa, both coercion and cooperation are necessary and complementary means, and that to regard them as mutually exclusive is to create a false dichotomy which ignores the complex reality of the situation. When non-violence is debated there tends to be a similar false dichotomy between non-violence and active protest: on a continuum between protest and capitulation, non-violence is equated with passive capitulation and submission. I believe the reverse to be true. Non-violence can form the basis of a powerful strategy that is constructive rather than destructive.

Hardly any topic in the South Africa political debate is more controversial and gives rise to more passion than the legitimacy of violence. In our violent society, non-violence has little or no appeal, either as a philosophy or as a strategy. Walter Wink (1987: 7) quotes an opponent of the government as saying 'The two dirtiest words in Black South Africa today are "nonviolence" and "reconciliation".'

Non-violence may seem to be a discredited approach in South Africa, particularly after so many years of suffering have not produced needed changes in the society. To the majority of people non-violence appears to be a weak evasion, a form of inaction, a luxury to be indulged by those not oppressed, even a calculated ploy by whites to keep blacks from demanding their due. Yet it remains a constructive approach to conflict, both as a philosophy for those firmly committed to it, and as a tactic for those seeking to change their situation.

Far from being a weak evasion, non-violence can be a strong basis for action. In the past it has been an important force in averting possible violence and in changing social structures and institutions which weighed heavily on the poor or powerless. It has been used historically to withdraw consent from an invading or tyrannical ruler, thus making a country ungovernable. Twentieth century exponents of non-violence include Gandhi, the Religious Society of Friends (Quakers), and Martin Luther King, who declared that 'unarmed truth is the most powerful thing in the universe'.

In 1906, under Gandhi's leadership, the first great passive resistance campaign in South Africa began in protest against the Transvaal Indian pass laws and it continued for years until these and other discriminating pieces of legislation were repealed.

The best known multi-racial non-violent direct action in South Africa took place in 1952 with the Defiance of Unjust Laws Campaign. The protesters, Africans and Indians, defied racially separate travel regulations and post office queues and informed the police whenever a group of non-violent volunteers was going to break a law. Over 8,000 people were arrested. Most of them chose to serve prison sentences rather than pay fines, and to read statements from the dock on why they had defied the law. The 1952 action failed to bring about desegregation or the lifting of other restrictions. Police brutality increased, leading to the Sharpeville massacre of 1960. It might be argued that the spirit of non-violent resistance resulted in the hardening of the government's attitude, and harsher laws, but leaders like Albert Luthuli believed that it constituted a turning point in the struggle for liberation by establishing a precedent for large-scale non-violent protest that gathered weight as it went, creating among Africans a new climate and a spirit of militant defiance.

In an interview published in the *Cape Times*, 22 July 1987, Bishop Desmond Tutu, Nobel Peace Prize laureate, was asked if he believed a programme of passive resistance could work in South Africa. His reply was indicative of widespread pessimism about the effectiveness of non-violence in the South African situation:

> My theory is that passive resistance presupposes a minimum level of morality so that those who are using it are hoping that somehow or other they will prick the consciences of a section of the community in which they live. Despite the difficulties of and dangers faced by Gandhi in India and King in the United States, they did know that in the end there was a constituency that would be morally outraged to see peacefully demonstrating people being made to run the gauntlet of bullwhips of the US police or the soldiers of the Raj.
>
> But let's come home to South Africa. The ANC used in the first 50 years of its existence conventional nonviolent methods, including a passive resistance campaign. And the response of the authorities, and of the white community basically, was an escalation of violence in the face of peaceful protest, culminating in the banning of the ANC and the PAC and the 1960 Sharpeville incident where, according to the evidence, many of the 69 people killed were shot in the back as they were running away.
>
> That is almost a paradigm that has been repeated over the years right up to the present. The authorities do not know how to handle peaceful protest, they are almost always seeking to provoke a violent response, which is the thing they know how to handle.

Tutu's answer includes arguments relating to non-violent opposition which are commonly heard in South Africa. 'We tried it and it did not work' has become a predictable reaction. But an abhorrence of the rising violence on all sides and the willingness to continue to try non-violent means of public protest, non-cooperation, and mass education have also increased. At another point in the interview, Bishop Tutu reiterates the call for effective non-violent action to be taken against the South African government. Recognition that the state is stronger than its opponents in its access to the means of violence and that it might, therefore, prefer violent opposition, has also become more widespread. The picture that emerges is one of frustration at the ineffectiveness of non-violence, coupled with a recognition that it might well be the only way for the majority.

Non-violent methods *have been* and *are being* used extensively in South Africa. When Dr Walter Wink asked participants at workshops in South Africa which tactics had been most successful in the last two years, they produced a remarkably long list of non-violent actions:

> labor strikes, slow-downs, sit-downs, stoppages and stay-aways; bus

boycotts, consumer boycotts and school boycotts; funeral demonstrations; non-cooperation with government-appointed functionaries; non-payment of rent; violation of government bans on peaceful meetings; defiance of segregation orders on beaches and in restaurants, theatres, and hotels; and the shunning of black police and soldiers. This is probably the largest grassroots eruption of diverse nonviolent strategies in a single struggle in human history! Yet these students, and many others we interviewed, both black and white, failed to identify these tactics as nonviolent, and even bridled at the word.

(Wink 1987: 4)

Force is on the side of the state. To quote Sheena Duncan, ex-president of the Black Sash, in 1983, 'The taking up of arms is most unproductive because the state knows how to meet violence with militarized response. There is no way that violence can defeat the state on its own ground. On sheer practicalities, it is a hopeless method' (South African Council of Churches 1983: 2). This view is becoming more widespread inside South Africa. This pragmatic view also recognizes that those in power may welcome violent opposition as a reason for tightening the existing apparatus of control. Non-violent resistance techniques make it more difficult for the government to explain away or justify its own high-handed or violent methods, either to foreign governments and diplomats or to its own constituency.

The tactical argument for non-violent action has still another aspect, one that brings it closer to the moral viewpoint, namely the relation of the means used to the nature of the end result. Violent struggles, where they do lead to success, tend to be followed by the concentration of power in the hands of those who control the means of violence. There is a lack of democracy inherent in violence. In contrast, non-violent struggles tend to diffuse power through the population as a whole. Once a population knows the techniques of non-violent resistance and the power it can wield, it becomes far more difficult to oppress them.

The non-violent approach combines pressure and cooperation. Its goals are both justice and peace — complementary goals, complementary means.

Civil disobedience and conscientious affirmation

Much if not most of the behaviour of agents is motivated by the wish to improve a situation, to right a wrong, or to remove an injustice. Thus there is a real danger that concerned individuals may become obsessed with fighting the evil in society, and that there is insufficient support for the good and positive elements. I note a distinct tendency in this direction in certain activist programmes and campaigns.

Approaches to Handling Conflict

There is an unfortunate negative element in any protest campaign against unjust governments and policies. Civil disobedience and conscientious objection are negative by definition — to disobey or object. As a form of non-violent protest and a method to bring about change, civil disobedience deserves support. When a system is intransigent and laws remain rigid, civil disobedience can be a powerful force. But there are two aspects in the concept that cause me concern. First, the negative element, which may easily overshadow fundamental, positive motivation. My second concern is about the mass nature of political campaigns. In this kind of activity individual judgement and commitment often become subordinate to mass emotion or even charismatic leadership. My plea is for a more positive response, and, more particularly, for *conscientious affirmation*.

Until recently we had several laws in South Africa which forbade intimate relations and inter-marriage between whites and blacks, as well as visits of white people to African townships without permits. Expression of inter-racial fellowship in certain cases was, therefore, illegal. Within this context I made a plea for a positive response of conscientious affirmation of inter-racial fellowship. This did not necessarily require breaking any laws, but certainly many customs. It required affirmative demonstration of fellowship, love, tolerance, and commitment to peace and justice. Our consciences, rather than custom or law, should dictate the affirmation of our fellowship across racial lines. The motivation is positive: the promotion of fellowship.

While civil disobedience is largely concerned with challenging immoral and unjust laws, conscientious affirmation is concerned with personal commitment. It is true that such a commitment may result in a brush with the law, just as in the case of civil disobedience, but such a clash depends upon the nature of the law and its application, and is not the major and direct object of the action. While civil disobedience and conscientious affirmation may, under certain conditions, require similar forms of behaviour, there is a marked difference in basic motivation. Civil disobedience is directed at what is wrong in society. Conscientious affirmation is concerned primarily with promoting what is right in society.

Support for conscientious affirmation was expressed by the Religious Society of Friends (Quakers) in South Africa a number of years ago and, at the annual conference of the South African Council of Churches in 1970, the following motion submitted by the Quaker participants was adopted:

> This conference is aware of many restrictions of interracial contact in our society. We find some of these restrictions morally so objectionable that we cannot obey them with clear conscience. We therefore

appreciate that many of our members may find that the affirmation of fellowship across racial lines is not possible within the law. We want to confirm that we support those of our members who commit themselves to conscientious affirmation of interracial fellowship. While it is difficult to make collective decisions binding others, we want to give moral encouragement to individuals and groups who are committed to such action.

The conference that accepted this motion did not accept another motion calling for massive civil disobedience. The delegates were not ready for such mass action. Perhaps one can make a case for conscientious affirmation as a training phase for orderly civil disobedience.

A good example of such conscientious affirmation of inter-racial fellowship was the small group of black and white American and South African Quakers and colleagues who decided in 1980 to travel together in a railway coach reserved for blacks only. Their intention was not primarily to commit civil disobedience but to travel together and to share experiences with black South Africans. People in their coach talked freely with them. The Quakers told each conductor, and then several policemen, that they did not mean to cause trouble but wanted to stay together. Eventually they were taken off the train to the nearest police station, cheered and encouraged by fellow passengers. After they had explained the spirit in which they had committed this illegal act the commandant said: 'You may ride together on the train but next time please notify us', and they were allowed to proceed on the next train. The story appeared in the newspapers and in an editorial denouncing petty apartheid. It was felt by Quakers that it might have a public impact, encouraging others to follow their consciences and perhaps resist apartheid by being together naturally.

Ideological commitment

The siege mentality

A pragmatic approach known as 'verligtheid' prevails among dominant politicians led by the State President. Their major motivating forces are no longer the Verwoerdian apartheid ideology but more pragmatic considerations about the maintenance of law and order, the increase in production (especially in a free market economic system) and the maintenance of 'civilized western standards'. In short, the pragmatists have come to realize that if (as whites) they want to retain any power, they have to share it with blacks. In the case of an election victory by Treurnicht of the Conservative Party the winner will take all. Power will not be shared with the National Party. But Nationalist leaders will most likely share power with black leaders in a new multi-racial government dominated by blacks. To what extent this intellectual, rational insight will prevail over traditional prejudices is not clear.

Not all adherents to apartheid ideology have left the National Party. Not even the verligtes can free themselves easily from the social forces that have shaped their views for so many generations. As Alan Paton has put it so aptly: P.W. Botha does not only have to face the right wing in the Conservative Party but also in his own party — and in his own heart. The National Party has retained many followers and a number of prominent leaders who are seemingly still motivated by the primary aim of maintaining white identity and protecting white privilege. This group adheres to the idea of white *baasskap* (superiority) and is not particularly interested in a negotiated settlement.

Improved communication will only help if there is a willingness to listen and learn with an open mind. Unfortunately, this is seldom possible in political conflict which usually has strong ideological content. Values, beliefs, and perceptions tend to exacerbate conflict, and ideologies such as race discrimination, apartheid, capitalism and communism may motivate people to act independently of their objective structural social positions or interests.

Ideological commitment usually leads to excessive intolerance, oversimplifications, polarization, and refusal to compromise or reconcile. In fact, the ideologization of conflict usually leads to its intensification because of the deep emotional investment tied into the basic values and beliefs. Adherents are not willing to subject their ideologies to critical analysis.

> Mediating ideologised conflict is a long, slow process. It would include the encouragement of contact between groups to erode polarisation and over-simplification and to build trust, as well as attempts to de-ideologise the conflict by focusing attention on objective aspects of the situation and by trying to remove the fear and insecurity that cause over-reliance on ideology. It is important to emphasise actual objective needs and de-emphasise ideological differences or interests.
> (Burton 1968: 50)

In South Africa the extent to which apartheid has become an ideology inhibits rational analysis and handling of political and economic problems. Now that there are signs of the waning of apartheid ideology in the establishment, new ideologies and counter-ideologies are emerging to meet psychological needs.

A lessening fear of colour and of blacks is making room for fear of communism and Russian imperialism. These alien forces are seen as constituting a 'total onslaught' on South Africa. 'That South Africa is the prize objective in the Soviet bid to control Southern Africa is an established fact', claimed the South African Broadcasting Corporation (SABC) in an editorial on 4 July 1983. This statement is the essence of the perception of the 'total onslaught'. It is seen as a communist-inspired, ideologically motivated struggle, aiming at the overthrow of the constitutional order and its replacement by a communist-oriented and subject black government. The liberation movement is seen as a tool of Communist Russia.

The para-military notion of a 'total onslaught' on the established order consisted not only of military aspects but also had political, diplomatic, economic, semantic, cultural, and psychological dimensions. The co-ordination of a defensive strategy had to incorporate all facets of South African society, thus generating the total strategy. As P.W. Botha explained in the *Defence White Paper* in 1977:

> The process of ensuring and maintaining the sovereignty of a state's authority in a conflict situation has, through the evolution of warfare, shifted from a purely military to an integrated national action. . . The resolution of a conflict in the times in which we now live demands interdependent and coordinated action in all fields — military, psychological, economic, political, sociological, technological, diplomatic, ideological, cultural, etc. . .
>
> (quoted in Moss 1980: 7)

The development of the total strategy required a close alliance between the government and the defence force and provided justification for the integration of the military into the governmental process. Since the 'total onslaught' was seen to be largely inspired by communist ideology and supported Russian imperialism, the total strategy was naturally directed against communism. Active support for the western-style market oriented economy became an important factor in the protection of 'civilized' western standards in South Africa.

The total national strategy was defined in the 1977 White Paper as 'the comprehensive plan to utilise all the means available to a state according to an integrated pattern in order to achieve the national aims within the framework of the specific policies'. Mass mobilization of the public in support of the government's total strategy was vigorously campaigned for by mass media, especially in editorial comment on the SABC:

> But — as emphasised by General Malan (the Minister of Defence) — the ANC terrorist has no conscience as far as his choice of targets or weapons is concerned. His goal is the whole country and the

entire population. And it is the main advantage of the terrorist — his ability as a clandestine operator to strike unexpectedly at vulnerable targets — which must be recognised and countered by the adoption of security as a general public obligation. Realistically speaking, it is the responsibility of organisations and individuals at all levels to play their part towards the overall security of their country.

While the South African government and conservative media continue with their efforts to excite public opinion against the 'total onslaught', allegedly orchestrated from Moscow, reputable scholars warn against this misperception. Recognized authorities in relatively conservative establishment-oriented institutions argue convincingly that Soviet policy-making does not emanate from a monolith and that policy concerning southern Africa is largely the preserve of lower levels of the Soviet bureaucracy.

In a recent paper Professor John Barratt, Director-General of the South African Institute of International Affairs (1988: 8), rejects the simplistic view of the total onslaught and calls for the clarification of our thinking on the so-called Soviet threat:

> There is also a need to clarify our thinking on the so-called Soviet threat. There is a widely held view among whites, promoted by official spokesmen, that we are defending the region against Soviet expansionism, and that the Soviets have been behind all regional problems and all hostile acts against South Africa. One does not have to regard the Soviet Union as a benevolent intervener in the region to reject such a simplistic view, which is not supported by the evidence and which surely cannot be the considered view of the government. In this view, as publicly expressed, several of the neighbour governments are simply depicted as Soviet puppets, and this propaganda is obviously not conducive to cooperation with such governments. If Pretoria is serious about promoting co-operative relations in the region and settling differences over security and other issues, then it needs public support for its dealings with the responsible governments in each of our neighbour states. To this end the public needs a more sophisticated and balanced analysis of the Soviet role in the region in official statements and from the government-controlled media. This is even more necessary now that Soviet policy is undergoing a change, as mentioned earlier.

Dr Philip Nel, director of the Institute for Soviet Studies at the University of Stellenbosch cites several White Papers and Nationalist Cabinet Ministers who argue that Soviet involvement in southern Africa 'is underpinned by a long-term Soviet desire to gain control over southern Africa in order to deny the "capitalist" world this region's mineral resources' (1988: 34). The 1982 White Paper states that 'the USSR strives to extend its influence to this area by assisting terrorist organisations such as Swapo and the South African ANC, by creating unrest and exploiting the situation, and by making use of surrogate forces such as the Cubans' (1988: 34).

Dr Nel argues that there is 'no credible evidence which suggests that Soviet involvement in southern Africa is compelled by a burning desire to control the mineral wealth of the region and especially that of South Africa (1988: 41). He echoes Prof Barratt's plea for a more informed opinion about Soviet policies.

The communist connection of the ANC is not in doubt. There is an alliance between the ANC and the South African Communist Party dating back several decades. This alliance is reinforced by the continued banning of the ANC and the lack of Western support. It is not the result of a commitment of the ANC to communist principles. The ANC is not a front organization of the communists, but an ally. Government spokesmen have on various occasions demanded that the ANC denounce communism and sever their communist links as prerequisites for negotiation. However, the ANC can obviously not be expected to renounce unconditionally its allies of several decades. The government will have to accept these connections and learn to live and compete with them. The most efficient way of reducing communist influence in the ANC would be to extend the friendship of the West and to unban it, so that it can develop its own independent power base in South Africa where it has the support of millions of non-communists and Christians.

The boycott mentality

Whether or not to participate in government-created political, economic, or social systems has been a source of intense conflict in South Africa. The issue concerns public functions, sports events, para-statal bodies, and forms of local and national government. Refusal to participate, withholding support and, especially, developing alternative systems can be powerful strategic tools. However, disagreement about how and when to use these tools remains a serious source of division among opponents of the government.

In South Africa an emotional revulsion against the 'system' has become so dominant that a mentality of 'total boycott' or total 'isolation' has developed in the extra-parliamentary opposition. Withdrawal has become a way of life, an end in itself. This boycott mentality (similar to that which has developed among anti-apartheid activists overseas) has generally led to a refusal to make any meaningful input into the political processes of the country.

Anti-apartheid organizations abroad are characterized by attitudes of despair and cynicism and a judgemental approach. This results in a refusal to do or contribute anything positive or constructive; every action is aimed at destroying the present evil, fighting apartheid, opposing the oppressor and bringing down the government. The primary motivating force is not the search for justice in South Africa but the wish to retaliate, to punish the evil-doer, to take revenge. Conditional sanctions, strikes, boycotts, and other withholding actions are valuable and efficient strategies in the political struggle. But when a boycott becomes an end in itself, a principle and not a strategy, it no longer constitutes a constructive approach to the accommodation of conflict.

International sanctions in perspective

To repeat may main theme, coercion (sanctions and even violence) and co-operation (negotiation) are complementary aspects of the communication process between contending groups (even between warring factions or nations). These situations are never stable. For relationships between contending groups to work towards both stability and the possibility of peaceful change, there should be a balance between coercion and co-operation.

Sanctions are an important instrument of foreign political pressure, both national and supra-national. Sanction is a term borrowed from Roman Law (*sanctio*, punishment). In modern international law, the term is interpreted as 'a punitive action by one state against another, designed to force a change of policy without resorting to overt aggression' (Braun and Weiland 1987: 3).

In international sanctions, the actors are, as a rule, national governments or international organizations, in a position to exert pressure on a target state. The target group is normally the government and its social power base. Braun and Weiland (1987: 4) argue that while the state may be the target, and the intention may be to change its behaviour and attitudes, in South Africa the black majority may be affected as severely or even more severely.

Comprehensive sanctions refer to a wide range of measures implemented simultaneously. In extreme instances they may result in an economic blockade imposed and enforced by military means. Selective sanctions refer to specific measures. These can be classified in the following categories:

Political and *diplomatic* sanctions include reducing or severing diplomatic relations and refusal of entry. *Cultural* sanctions include restricting or breaking off cultural and sporting relations and academic and scientific exchanges.

Military sanctions include arms embargos, abrogation of co-operative agreements, and, in severe cases, a military blockade. *Economic* sanctions are generally regarded as the most effective because of international economic interdependence. In applying sanctions to South Africa this was the most popular choice. The economic boycott campaign has come to dominate the international sanction campaign against South Africa. Economic sanctions can be divided into four types (Braun and Weiland 1987: 4):

Trade sanctions aim at restricting or stopping imports and exports between the target state and the sanctioning or sender states, as well as trade relations between the target state and third parties. *Financial* sanctions are intended to influence the flow of foreign capital into and the volume of capital in the target state. Their aim is to impair both the willingness and the possibility to invest and, above all, reduce the liquidity of the economy as a whole. The two concepts most commonly used in connection with South Africa are disinvestment and divestment (Braun and Weiland 1987: 4-5; Orkin 1986: 17).

Sanctions on *services* are intended to put a strain on international relations. They affect mainly traffic, for example, the refusal to grant landing rights to South African airline companies, the closure of land and sea routes, restrictions on tourism (visa requirements), restrictions on communication (mail, media, flow of information). Sanctions on the *transfer* of *technology* are intended to prevent the international exchange of technological knowledge and technical experience.

The whole range of sanctions has not been fully and rationally considered because the international boycott campaign has acquired an emotional character and lacks a rational plan of action. Furthermore, sanctions against South Africa are often largely determined by domestic policies in sender states and the psychological needs of the actors themselves.

The sanctions debate in many countries, such as in the United States and the United Kingdom, has been initiated for a great part by pressure groups and popular movements that exploit international issues for domestic gain or ideological goals. The means used do not necessarily relate to the stated goals for South Africa but are often linked to domestic goals or party political advantage.

Relatively strong support for the anti-apartheid and sanctions movements exists, however, in countries such as Denmark, Ireland, the United Kingdom, the Netherlands and the United States, where there is a genuine concern for universal human rights. In these countries popular organizations arise that put pressure on their governments to make a moral commitment to justice and to identify with the oppressed in all parts of the world. This underlies their stand on sanctions.

Given the complexity of social forces underlying sanctions, the campaign should be assessed in terms of goals and major motivating forces.

Approaches to Handling Conflict

Political objectives determine the nature and range of sanctions adopted. These range from demands for marginal adaptations in government policy to fundamental structural changes in the socio-economic system.

Given a certain vagueness of goals and strong disagreements in the international community about both goals and means, the international sanctions campaign lacks unity, direction and rational planning. Crowds involved in large demonstrations and meetings probably have vague ideas about goals and appropriate means, apart from bringing down an oppressive regime and weakening or destroying multi-national companies through boycotts.

Over past decades there has been a close ideological affinity between many economic boycott movements and those groups that attack two of the major evils of the current capitalist system: the exploitation of workers, and involvement in the military-industrial complex in Western countries, especially in the United States. Those expounding the cause of the poor, the exploited, the powerless labourer, especially in the Third World, have begun to look for causes in the interplay of big business and the arms-related economy. Similarly, groups disturbed not only by the escalating arms build-up but by actual warfare, seemingly induced by the military-industrial complex, have targetted big business and especially trans-national companies.

Organizers of the economic boycott campaign found fruitful soil among people genuinely concerned about the exploitation of the poor and the threat of war. Individuals who are agitated about social and political issues of exploitation and violence are becoming accustomed to thinking first of pressuring the business sector to achieve social change. The unfortunate result of this development has been that big business and not the South African government has become the major target.

Moral commitment to universal human rights has been replaced by moral indignation about injustices and anger towards the oppressors, with resultant punitive action to give expression to this indignation and anger. This tends to give the boycott an *expressive* rather than an instrumental character. It becomes the goal itself, rather than merely a means. Commitment to boycott as a strategy tends to over-simplify the issues, to narrow the scope of operation, and to increase intolerance. Moral indignation shapes a negative short-term goal — that of destroying the object of indignation.

While this book is primarily concerned with negotiation, mediation, and third party intervention in pursuit of peace and reconciliation, I have argued in Chapter 1 that there can be no peace without justice. I acknowledge the role of coercion in the pursuit of justice and argue in this chapter that pressures, including sanctions and even violence, should be seen as complementary to co-operation, including negotiation. This assumption of complementarity, the technique of the carrot and the stick, supports the belief that sanctions against South Africa will force or encourage the government to enter into negotiations with credible leaders of the majority of South Africans. Such negotiations should lead to full representation of black people in the central government, in a system generally described as majority rule.

To achieve this goal and to assure that sanctions complement negotiations, sanctions should meet the following five conditions:

1. Sanctions should be non-violent, as far as possible. I formulate this condition as a committed Quaker, but also with caution, having accepted above that forms of violence can be interpreted as complementary to negotiation. While accepting violence as endemic, I will continue my search for non-violent or, at least, less violent forms of behaviour. I must also repeat my argument that violence includes structural violence. Government policies and economic measures cause psychological and mental as well as physical harm to individuals and groups and prohibit their full development.

    Economic boycotts that will cause economic recession, unemployment, hunger, starvation and death are an obvious form of institutional violence. Calculations about the potential harm that will be done to people within South Africa and the neighbouring countries vary but there is no doubt that a successful boycott will be devastating. And the whites will be able to ensure that the blacks will suffer most. When foreign investments declined after the Soweto protest of 1976, Pretoria decided to reduce imports, maximize exports, and limit growth. This was done with almost no harm to whites, while one million Africans lost their jobs. It has been estimated that several African states would be ruined economically if sanctions were applied effectively against South Africa.

    Leaders of frontline states are ambiguous in their pronouncements. Political leaders from Mozambique and Botswana have made it clear that to support sanctions would be tantamount to suicide. It would cause excessive suffering which could not be justified.

    The violence of economic boycott has been spelled out by President Kenneth Kaunda: 'But economic sanctions if firmly applied . . . are only more humane than war in the sense that starving someone to death is more humane than shooting him' (Kaunda 1980: 65).

2. Sanctions should be selective and based on a rational cost-benefit analysis. I have listed earlier a wide range of political, diplomatic, cultural, military, and economic measures that could be implemented without causing the massive unemployment implied in most of the current proposals for economic boycott. These restrictions could

have a serious impact on the whites and on political decision-makers without substantially affecting the blacks. For example, it is generally agreed that the sports boycott of the past two decades has been extremely successful in removing race barriers in sport in South Africa. Unfortunately, rational cost-benefit analysis is absent in most pro-sanction lobbies.

3. While it is accepted that apartheid, as a violation of universal human rights, is of concern to the international community and that pressure from outside is justified, it would be in the country's interest that pressures on the establishment and on the government should come from internal rather than external sources. There is a distinct danger that the involvement of superpowers may reduce the contending parties within South Africa to pawns on the international chessboard. I believe that it would serve a better purpose to focus on building up opposition groups within South Africa, such as trade unions, rather than to focus on destroying the ruling group, business and industry and, by implication, the country's infrastructure. Consider the difference between a boycott implemented by foreigners that forces a multi-national company to withdraw from South Africa and deprives Africans of their jobs, and a strike called by Africans against that company, demanding better working conditions and political rights.

Africans need bargaining power and through their employment they are building up powerful trade unions. In simple terms it is better to support and empower a trade union than to destroy a company.

4. This argument leads to the next condition: sanctions should be constructive rather than destructive. Some sanctions could be constructive in consequences even if not clearly so in form. Andrew Young, former United States Ambassador to the United Nations, made a convincing case for closing all air traffic routes to and from South Africa, coupled with a boost for substitute air traffic with the front-line states. He outlined all the advantages for both front-line states and South Africans of such a move. Under the heading 'To Rouse South Africans, Clamp a Ban on Air Links', he wrote in the *International Herald Tribune* of 13 August 1986: 'An embargo on air travel to and from South Africa is one sanction that would be more redemptive than punitive, more creative than destructive. Its main effect would be on those citizens who are most powerful. It would do little or no harm to poor blacks, whom outsiders suddenly seem so concerned about when sanctions are discussed.'

5. Sanctions should be coupled with conditions which are clear and can be met; conditions that demand, and have a chance of obtaining, improved conditions in southern Africa, rather than a demand

for the immediate abdication of the present government.

I have dealt with pressure and sanctions as means of bringing conflicting parties together to arrange a negotiated settlement. I have tried to spell out some conditions which may affect the impact of sanctions upon the country. If sanctions are seen as complementary to negotiation, and care is taken that pressures in fact drive the parties to the negotiation table and not *away* from it, careful attention will then have to be given to the process of negotiation. Given the state of polarization in South Africa, direct communication in the form of negotiation is difficult, perhaps impossible, at this stage. There is a need for intermediaries. I therefore turn in Chapter 6 to third party intervention and mediation.

Chapter six

Third Party Intervention

The need for intervention

The South African political climate is fraught with obstacles to meaningful and direct communication and negotiation between the government and broadly-based black leadership. There are seemingly irreconcilable differences between the respective positions on power, equality, the pace of change and apartheid, and each side is threatened with a serious erosion of its political base if publicly seen to acknowledge the legitimacy of the other.

Peacemakers are always suspect on both sides and, unless there is a strong enough support group, most people do not opt for the middle way for fear of falling between two stools. The Reverend Ian Paisley of Northern Ireland has expressed his aversion for the middle group very clearly: 'Bridge-builders and traitors are alike, they both go over to the other side.'

In Chapter 5 I indicated ways in which inappropriate and destructive handling of conflict by the major political groups in South Africa has exacerbated the conflict and contributed towards further polarization. Political observers believe the situation has deteriorated significantly in 1988, that the government's reform programme has been shelved, and that there are virtually no prospects for negotiation between the government and the mass-based opposition groups, including the UDF and the ANC, between the establishment and the extra-systemic opposition.

In situations where direct communication between conflicting parties is absent, it becomes necessary for a third party to intervene to facilitate communication. South Africans should take note of encouraging developments in several other countries. In recent years in many areas of social life, alternative dispute settlement mechanisms, often involving the intervention of mediators, have had notable success in helping disputants to come to a mutually satisfactory settlement outside the court system. Less apparent is the success of intervention efforts to resolve serious disputes at an international level. However, recent cases like the

Camp David Accord (1978), the Lancaster House settlement of the Zimbabwean conflict (1979), and ongoing arms control negotiations between the USA and the USSR, point to the possibility that seemingly intractable international problems can be constructively addressed and sometimes even settled through *skillful third-party intervention*. Intermediary initiatives have also been launched in recent years by groups of countries, such as the British Commonwealth and the Western Contact Group, in attempts to resolve regional conflicts in southern Africa.

In this chapter I discuss aspects of intervention, with special emphasis on constructive contributions by informal or unofficial intermediaries acting in facilitating or mediating roles, with illustrations from my own experiences.

Third-party intervention should not be seen as a distinct category of behaviour but rather as a role assumed at certain times by certain people. It forms part of a wider continuum of behaviour patterns in which the intervener adopts a variety of roles and techniques (Bercovitch 1984: 16). Intervention can be either neutral or partisan. The purpose of neutral intervention is usually to mediate between conflicting parties, to improve communication and to promote a negotiated settlement.

Partisan intervention could be motivated by a variety of reasons: to advocate the cause of one party or to assist it in the conflict, to protect the *status quo*, or to assist and empower the weaker party. Strategies of partisan intervention range from repression — the most anti-change or establishment-supporting option — to generating conflict (the strongest pro-change option), depending on the opinions, attitudes, and convictions of the intervener.

Mediation refers to intervention in a dispute or negotiation by an acceptable, impartial, and neutral third party to assist contending parties to reach a mutually acceptable settlement or truce. Mediation and negotiation are thus closely allied. Mediation is, in a sense, an extension of negotiation because it brings an added dimension, a third party, into the process.

Mediation and negotiation are, however, two fundamentally different activities. The negotiator acts on behalf of an interest group as an adversary in a conflict situation, while the mediator is a neutral third party intervening between conflicting groups or adversaries. While the negotiator takes a stand on behalf of his group, the mediator is impartial and has no vested interest in the outcome of the dispute.

In practice most of us engage in both activities at one time or another, depending on the occasion, the circumstances, and our own dispositions. No wonder these two roles are often confused in the public mind. When Archbishop Desmond Tutu sees the State President does he do so as a negotiator on behalf of his own people, or as a mediator between the government and the churches?

We often read in the papers about prominent people 'mediating' in community and political conflict. Nearly all of these are examples of partisan intervention. While I encourage and praise such efforts, and while there is ample evidence that they often contribute quite significantly towards better understanding and better relations, it is misleading to refer to them as mediation. If these efforts fail, as they sometimes do, the public may argue that we have tried mediation and it did not work.

I therefore accept the morality and sincerity of intervention, including partisan intervention. But the true mediator must be acceptable to *all* parties. Prominent advocates of certain political views or ideologies, whether conservative, liberal or radical, cannot mediate in conflicts between *witdoeke* (pro-government vigilantes) and comrades in Cape Town, or between Inkatha and the UDF in Natal.

While status and prestige can be helpful qualities in a mediator, such qualities may under certain conditions be impediments. When Coretta King, widow of Martin Luther King, came to South Africa for the consecration of Archbishop Desmond Tutu, she attempted in vain to play the role of a mediator between the government and the blacks. She backed down under pressure from blacks and failed to keep an appointment with the State President. When her almost tearful figure appeared next to the victorious Winnie Mandela on the front pages of the world's papers, observers commented that this proved there was no room for mediation.

This observation, however, is based on a misinterpretation of Mrs King's role in South Africa. For South African blacks neither she nor her late husband are symbols of peacemaking, but of protest, albeit non-violent. They symbolize the newly-gained confidence and self-respect of black people. For Coretta King to attempt to act as a peacemaker would threaten this symbolism, especially if this attempt came at the moment of great jubilation with the consecration of a black person as the head of a conventional 'white' church.

Not all conflict situations call for mediation. Major social and political changes are usually brought about by varying degrees of confrontation. Mediation must not be used to hold back the inevitable process of change. In political conflict gross asymmetry of power inhibits the negotiation process and is detrimental to a lasting negotiated settlement. In such situations there may be greater need for an activist who helps latent conflict to become manifest, who promotes the process of empowerment as an important pre-condition for negotiation.

If a community has generated the energy to confront authority and demand legitimate change it would be wasteful to defuse the situation before a strong case had been made by the protesting party. It would be counter-productive for the mediator to enter this sort of situation too soon, or at the request of the establishment only, or even if asked to come in by a few faint-hearted members of the community. Under such conditions partisan intervention on behalf of the weaker party is required together with, or even prior to, neutral intervention.

In situations where fruitless violence is occurring, however, mediation to arrange a truce becomes a priority. This applies particularly to what has become known as township violence in South Africa. On several occasions the UDF and Inkatha have agreed to accept mediation as a kind of interim measure, provided it is restricted to the reduction of violence and does not compromise them on any fundamental principles.

Empowerment encompasses a range of developmental features in addition to building up of economic, social, and political power bases. These include education, training, confidence-building, community organization, and leadership development. Empowerment must be a democratic, grassroots process. Power that is conferred by the state on black leaders lacks legitimacy and is not respected.

Qualities and tasks of mediators

Neutrality and concern

One of the most important qualities of a mediator is neutrality and impartiality. This does not mean that the mediator has no personal values or opinions, but that he does not take sides on that particular issue in which he is mediating. In many cases it seems almost impossible for an individual to be completely impartial — there is a tendency to lean towards one or another party. For that reason a team of mediators is often used so that possible individual biases can be balanced out.

Neutrality does not come easily. Most people tend to take sides. It is especially difficult for people who have normative notions of behaviour, and who are inclined to regard behaviour as being right or wrong. Refraining from judgement is especially difficult for those who attribute behaviour to individual motivation and personality characteristics rather than to environmental forces and those who tend to hold people individually responsible for behaviour that is socially determined. Many people search instinctively for individual 'culprits' behind unacceptable policies and actions. Lawyers, rigid pacifists, and militants make poor mediators.

Neutrality and detachment can, however, be interpreted as lack of feeling, care and concern by suffering, deprived or oppressed parties, parties that believe they have been wronged, or parties that are or feel threatened. This is essentially true of black South Africans, but it applies to many other groups including white South Africans as the minority group in the country and the Nationalist Government as being responsible for our status as a pariah in the family of nations.

An acceptable mediator must empathize with all parties in conflict. The use of the term 'resolution' has given rise to the fear that inequalities, injustices and violations of human rights may be ignored or smoothed over by intermediaries who undertake peacemaking for ulterior motives, determined to come up with solutions. Academics with grand plans they want to try out to provide material for books, or foreigners who build up reputations as successful mediators and win international acclaim are suspect and often unacceptable.

Expression of concern is not always reconcilable with the necessary quality of impartiality of the mediator. Can concern for the oppressed be expressed without sacrificing this impartiality and without estranging the oppressor? I believe so, provided that concern for suffering is distinguished from preferential support for any one party in the conflict. Genuine concern can be expressed for a group without supporting any of its particular stands, goals, policies, or methods. Adam Curle, experienced international Quaker mediator (1986: 19), explains that expressions of shock and horror about atrocities may seem to one party to imply sympathy with the enemy. He suggests: 'Perhaps the best approach is to express sorrow, but in a way that suggests no blame except to the practice of war which makes such tragedies, committed by either side, inevitable.' He argues that it is through this 'concerned impartiality' that mediators are able to remain on good terms with both sides.

Another Quaker mediator described this attitude as 'balanced partiality'. 'A more appropriate though paradoxical description might be a balanced partiality — that is, they listened sympathetically to each side, trying to put themselves in the other party's place. The evidence is clear that they were perceived as sympathetic listeners on both sides' (Yarrow in Berman and Johnson 1977: 99). This approach is often possible in situations of extreme violence where both parties are suffering from material and human losses, as in violent confrontations between opposing parties in Natal. In most incidents one of the parties usually suffers greater losses than the other, but the series of incidents offers opportunities for expression of concern towards both sides by the intermediary.

Injury and death caused by political violence in South Africa provide ample cause for public statements by concerned people such as church leaders. But, because of polarization, the occasions at which these statements are made, the media through which they are conveyed to the public, their content and tone almost invariably reflect the partisan political stands of these leaders. Conservative or pro-establishment church leaders show their greatest horror at the acts of the protest or liberation movements, and their deepest concern and sympathy for their victims; while anti-government church leaders express their greatest horror at the acts of the security forces and their deepest concern and sympathy for their victims.

The extent to which expressions of selective concern contribute towards further polarization came home to me after the cross-border attack of the South African Defence Force (SADF) on Maseru in December 1982, followed by the bomb detonated by ANC supporters or agents in Pretoria on 20 May 1983 and the retaliatory attack by the SADF on Maputo three days later. These acts left victims on both sides and elicited numerous public statements and denunciations.

These events and the responses to them in both white and black circles, among conservatives and liberals, made me intensely aware of the spiral of polarization that is driving our country into rigidly opposed camps of mutual hatred and commitment to revenge. This element of revenge was evident in the public statements of both the ANC and the South African Government. On Monday, 23 May 1983, General Malan, Minister of Defence, stated in Parliament that 'the security forces of South Africa will revenge every drop of blood shed by the innocent — white, black or brown — with all the force at its disposal'. This attitude pervades our whole society. Blacks cheered when they heard of the Pretoria bomb, and so did whites when they heard of the revenge a few days later.

I could not help noticing in private conversations and in public statements by my colleagues and church leaders how the intensity of their responses reflected their political biases and reinforced polarization. In response to this situation I formulated a statement of concern which I intended to serve as a contribution towards conciliation. In this statement I expressed my disapproval of violence on both sides, my sympathy with the victims on both sides, my belief in the elements of goodwill on both sides, and my intention to make financial contributions to the victims on both sides.

This statement, together with a small donation, was conveyed both to the trustees of the State President's Fund in South Africa which was established to assist victims of terrorism, and to the Lesotho Christian Council which assisted victims of the SADF attack on Maseru. To my disappointment (but not to my surprise) this statement was deplored and attacked by colleagues and church leaders. Some accused me of supporting the terrorists and others of supporting apartheid, saying that the government should take care of its own victims!

My statement was also shared with black and white leaders of conflicting political views with whom I came into contact. The development of a relationship of trust with the African National Congress in exile, and with the establishment in subsequent years can largely be attributed to these expressions of impartial concern.

While I deplore selective concern based on partisan politics, I sympathize with selective concern based on humanitarian feelings. Bias towards the deprived and oppressed characterize all humanitarian intervention. Unofficial mediators usually have strong humanitarian motivations and a natural sympathy with the deprived or wronged. Quakers, internationally, have traditionally sided with the underdog and in South Africa interventions by British and South African Quakers have consistently been inspired by the plight of the underdog. During the Anglo-Boer War Quakers sympathized with the Boers and at present they assist blacks.

This kind of sympathy could easily lead to partisan intervention in the sense that the deprived are seen as morally right or superior and the oppressors are equated with evil. Mediation between oppressor and oppressed therefore presents a special challenge to mediators with strong humanitarian concerns. This was well described by a wise and elderly Quaker couple:

> The role of the peacemaker is beset with difficulties and he often is under attack from both sides. But Friends collectively must be concerned for and with everyone and perhaps particularly for those whose minority but power-holding position makes them stand condemned by the world at large. There is no particular virtue in helping the innocent; this is a natural human reaction. But to help the guilty requires grace. And to help them one must be in contact.
> (Letter from Shifa and Hugh Doncaster, 4 November 1977)

The Quaker belief that there is something of God in everyone is firmly based on the teachings of the Bible, it receives support from Christians and is a central belief in major world religions. There is an element of God in everyone, says Wink (1987: 55):

> There is no one, and surely no entire people, in whom the image of God has been utterly extinguished. Faith in God means believing that *anyone* can be transformed, regardless of the past. To write off whole groups of people as intrinsically racist and violent is to accept the very same premise that upholds apartheid.

The biblical understanding of the Powers (authorities) is that they are indeed fallen but not totally depraved. Even when they are repressive in the extreme they still embody something that must be honoured (Wink 1987: 61). Apart from theological truths, there are also practical considerations:

> To a certain extent the refusal to have interaction with enemies is a result of seeing the opposition as a monolith. We fail to note that the enemy camp is inevitably riddled with power struggles, fragmentation, back stabbing, personal vendettas, bureaucratic infighting and careerism, all of which conspire to prevent maximum efficiency in

oppression. Likewise we tend to freeze them in their current public postures, thus denying to them the possibility of making the very changes we are demanding of them.

(Wink 1987: 50-1)

The tendency to be biased towards the innovative, progressive stand as against the conservative preservation of the *status quo* is common among intellectuals and academics who also tend to favour the deprived, the underdog. This bias is clearly manifested in conflict and peace research and in the peace movement.

Tord Hoivik of the International Peace Institute in Oslo argued that social theory should serve the oppressed, not the oppressors (Gurr 1980: 13). Hoivik's stand is, however, based on the false assumption that rebels are always oppressed and are right, while rulers are always oppressors and are evil. Gurr points out that the scholar's first and fundamental obligation is to seek valid understanding and not to serve any particular interest group. The problem of bias in favour of the underdog is a serious one for mediators and facilitators, who must maintain their impartiality in order to function successfully.

Improve communication

Facilitators must remove blocks and distortions in the communication process so that mutual understanding may develop. Conflicts of interest are exacerbated by subjective phenomena which occur when existing conditions prevent effective communication or accurate assessments of costs and values, and consideration of alternative means and goals.

Parties to a conflict have exceedingly rigid ideas about the character and motives of their opponents, which are developed over years of conflict and biased information. Each party has a favourable image of itself and its behaviour and an unfavourable view of the other as treacherous. The distortion is obvious: no group could be so consistently evil-minded and inclined to violence as it is perceived by its enemies.

The mediator or conciliator facilitates exchange, suggests possible solutions, and assists the parties in reaching a voluntary agreement. I make a clear distinction, however, between mediation and facilitation. Facilitation is restricted to the facilitation of communication between conflicting parties. Unlike the mediator the facilitator does not suggest solutions or help the parties reach agreement and is primarily concerned with technical rather than moral issues: the improvement of communication rather than the promotion of solutions.

The mediator is usually motivated by a concern to reach a peaceful solution, consensus, conciliation, or some similar goal. He or she can claim neutrality regarding the stands taken by conflicting parties, but not regarding the outcome of the exercise. For the facilitator, facilitation of communication is an end in itself, in much the same way as one can pursue knowledge for the sake of knowledge or atomic power for the sake of power. The mediator is relatively more concerned with the use made of new insights gained from reliable communication, while the facilitator is primarily concerned with ensuring that the relevant parties gain accurate information, regardless of what use they make of it.

For these reasons a facilitator may, in situations of extreme polarization and intense suspicion, be more acceptable to conflicting parties than a mediator. The neutral and almost technical services of the facilitator would appear to be more functional than the assistance of a mediator, who is morally committed to peacemaking. I want to argue, therefore, that at this stage in South Africa we should consider facilitation as a first step before attempting mediation between the major contending parties.

In my experience with the South African establishment and the African National Congress (ANC) in exile, I have always maintained that I served as a facilitator assisting both parties to have meaningful communication and gain reliable information. I did not urge the parties to put the knowledge to good use or to make peace. It was up to them to decide how they would use these insights. This approach probably accounts for the positive responses I have had from both sides. The facilitator is less likely than the mediator to be seen as a meddler or a busybody, a preacher, or a conciliator. He or she does not offer or attempt to bring the parties together, but, obviously, should the parties be ready to take that step, the facilitator may well be an appropriate person to assist.

This is exactly what hapened when I was invited in 1985 to facilitate between the UDF and Inkatha in Natal. One party urged me to arrange a meeting and to make peace but the other party, which at that time felt strategically at a disadvantage, did not want any reconciliation, fearing that it would merely serve the purpose of maintaining the *status quo*, which from their point of view was unjust. The latter group wanted the assurance that justice would be done before there was any peacemaking. But, being the weaker party, they were suffering heavy losses through violence. They were willing to participate in any *ad hoc* effort to reduce physical violence. This wish gave rise to the idea of setting up a Joint Monitoring Committee and eventually a meeting was held to establish such a committee. In other words, while one party was unwilling to meet with the enemy for purposes of peacemaking, it was indeed willing to meet (almost by default) for a more specific strategic purpose. As an intermediary I was accepted as somebody who was providing a technical rather than moral service.

While reference is made in this book to foreign government intervention in South Africa, my focus is on unofficial diplomacy: something frequently practised by organizations like the World Council of

Churches, the International Red Cross, and the Religious Society of Friends. One reason for this focus is that this kind of diplomacy may help to pave the way for subsequent official mediation for which the parties are not yet ready. Another reason is that I have been involved in this kind of intervention and have relied heavily on my own experiences in writing this book.

Any involvement by local or outside governments or official bodies tends to give official status to the communication process between contending parties. This is exactly what the parties want to avoid when they are not ready for mediation. Such circumstances call for the quiet, informal services of 'unofficial diplomats', individuals without official status, power, or vested interest. Non-official mediators are not employed by or responsible to national governments or inter-governmental organizations. Michael Banks (1987: 23) concludes that:

> In recent years, reports of private diplomacy (carried out by Quaker representatives, respected businessmen and others), have shown that there are significant benefits to the parties in the conciliating, go-between role that non-political individuals can create for themselves.

While they have no political, economical, or military clout facilitators working as individuals have the freedom to be flexible, to disregard protocol, to suggest unconventional remedies or procedures, to widen or restrict the agenda or change the order of items, to propose partial solutions or package deals, to press the case for constructive initiatives or magnanimous gestures (Bailey 1985: 211). Such private initiatives may contribute to the alleviation of problems in communication. 'By providing auxiliary channels of communication, by serving as intermediaries between governments, by performing various third-party functions, including negotiating and mediating in conflict situations, and by contributing to a climate in which policy-makers can usefully work, private citizens may augment and facilitate official diplomacy' (Berman and Johnson 1977: 7)

> The intent of some of the individuals who initiate private efforts is to prepare the way for intergovernmental action, and often they act with the blessing or at least the knowledge of officials of governments or international organizations. When it suits their purposes, governments may support and use private channels.
> (Berman and Johnson 1977: 7)

Informal intermediaries often pave the way for official mediation and negotiation by carrying proposals, responses, and other messages between the parties, ensuring the flow of accurate and reliable information, interpreting and clarifying positions to minimize misunderstandings, to find ways to begin building trust, and to help to bring to the surface ideas, alternatives and options for resolving differences.

Identify issues and needs

The mediator or facilitator must help the parties to identify and to confront the issues in an analytical and rational way. He must also help to provide favourable circumstances in which to confront the issues. Parties to a conflict make things easier for themselves by simplifying issues and focusing on their own viewpoints, because this mobilizes their constituencies and gains support. But to strip a conflict of its complexity is to falsify it. One function of the facilitator or mediator is to help participants to acknowledge that they are enmeshed together in a complex and multi-dimensional problem.

In recent years international mediators and scholars have found that identification of needs, rather than values and interests, improves the chances of resolution of conflict. The theory of needs as developed by Maslow and others, stresses needs that cannot be curbed, socialized, or negotiated. This approach has been applied to conflict studies by prominent scholars like John Burton of the Centre for the Analysis of Conflict, and John Groom of the University of Kent. Arguing that the individual has certain basic needs not only in a physical sense (e.g. food and shelter), but also as a social unit (e.g. recognition and security), Burton (1979: 59) posits that:

> Needs describe those conditions or opportunities that are essential to the individual if he is to be a functioning and co-operative member of society, conditions that are essential to his development and which, through him, are essential to the organisation and survival of society.

There has been a shift in conflict resolution and settlement theory, away from the classical authoritarian approach of confrontation towards an approach that emphasizes the need for interaction between conflicting parties. This led to the acceptance of the idea that, in order to be effective, negotiations require some accommodation of the needs of the weaker party, where a power imbalance exists.

Concentrating on needs rather than on interests will assist the mediator in finding creative alternatives. The chances of finding a self-sustaining solution are, in this way, enhanced. It is important to note that conflicts over social needs are not of a zero-sum nature, since the increase in the security of one party will not automatically lead to an equal decrease in security for the other parties.

The mediator should point out to disputants that individuals (as part of groups) will always engage in 'pathological' and deviant behaviour, such as the unrestrained use of violence, if certain needs, sometimes expressed as independence struggles, struggles for national liberation or freedom struggles are not met. This consideration also points to the weakness of deterrence by threat or coercion in situations where these needs are being frustrated.

Having identified issues, interests, and needs the mediator must help to establish certain agreed norms for rational interaction, such as mutual respect, the use of persuasion rather than coercion, and the desirability of reaching a mutually satisfying agreement. 'Fair rules of procedure are valuable in any kind of discussion but are vital in conflicts' (Deutsch 1973: 385), where the perception that no rules apply too often prevails. In due course the mediator may help the parties to formulate solutions that are mutually acceptable and viable.

Helping parties to save face

In any situation of conflict and particularly in adversarial politics, parties go out of their way to embarrass their opponents whenever they change policy or admit past errors. Leaders want to avoid at all costs any appearance that they are backing down under pressure.

The mediator must help parties to determine what kind of solutions are acceptable and try to develop circumstances favourable for the implementation of proposed solutions. He must also help negotiators to make the agreement seem as prestigious and attractive as possible to all constituencies. Unless this is done, negotiators will not gain support for the agreement from their constituencies. Agreements which require shifts in publicly-held opinions, attitudes, and beliefs can be greatly facilitated if the person or the party is allowed to save face and to change with his self-esteem intact. Mediators should at all times be willing to take the blame for negotiations that break down and allow negotiators to take the credit for mediation that succeeds.

Mediators must respect the popular base of elected leaders and acknowledge tensions between their privately held views and their public statements. The sensitive mediator will sympathize with representatives of conflicting parties who are willing to make concessions and who say so in private negotiations, while they proclaim the opposite in public statements because their constituencies are not willing to make concessions. Mediators thus have to help leaders with the re-entry process, which involves selling the agreement to their constituencies.

Mediators may have helped to formulate solutions in the private negotiation process. Now they must help to develop circumstances favourable for the implementation of the proposed solutions. This introduces a controversial element in the role of mediators who, ideally, remain in the background.

Private and public roles of mediators

Mediators in real life are often also opinion makers. By reaching out to the public they extend the negotiation process to other levels of society and facilitate the acceptance of agreements. But the blurring of the roles of private, discreet mediators and public opinion-makers, however, causes severe tensions and can be highly controversial.

Confidentiality and even secrecy are essential conditions for mediation and facilitation between public bodies. Such confidentiality poses no problem for most professional mediators who are called in as neutral outsiders. Academics, such as the members of the Centre for the Analysis of Conflict, have produced numerous publications based on their experiences in international intervention without disclosing details of parties involved or their respective stands. Information can also be published after the event in a way that causes no embarrassment to either party.

Separation between the quiet, discreet, and private role of the detached mediator and the public (even aggressive) educational campaign of the opinion-maker is seldom possible for most South Africans who try to be both mediators and opinion makers. They bring contending leaders together and they also try to influence their constituencies.

There are sometimes convincing reasons for mediators to go public even during the process of intervention. Third parties can help in resolving disputes constructively to the extent that they are known and seen as prestigious. The mass media can help in this task by giving publicity to their work but, even more important, in helping to promote public opinion in favour of third party intervention and a negotiated settlement.

I believe the Eminent Persons Group (EPG), representing the British Commonwealth, maintained a healthy balance between their tasks of private mediation and public education. While many observers described their mission as a failure I have no doubt that they made an invaluable contribution, not only in formulating common ground between the parties, but especially by making both third party intervention and the idea of a negotiated settlement respectable in the public eye. What they achieved in public may have exceeded the benefits of their private negotiations with the respective leaders.

Another good example of the successful combination of private and public mediating activities is that of the Wiehahn Commission on labour legislation. Prof Nic Wiehahn and his colleagues were not commissioned to mediate but they systematically set out on a process of mediation, coupled with public education, knowing that this was the only way in which they could obtain the co-operation of the parties (especially the Nationalist government and business interests) or sell the proposals to the public. The way the Commission both sensitized and educated the parties can be seen in their programme of preparation. This involved press leakages on their proposals, public lectures, use of an in-house journal, publication of a labour relations study series to educate industrial relations practitioners, and a two-month trip overseas by Wiehahn to sell the report abroad. Compared with other government commissions that made progressive proposals, the Wiehahn commission was a great success.

I have experienced, and still do, a fairly serious dilemma and considerable ambivalence between my private role as facilitator and my public role as opinion-maker. My opinion-forming role is attached to my position as Director of an institute that promotes educational and training programmes in conflict management on local, regional, and national levels. Promoting these programmes requires not only provision of an infrastructure and organizational facilities but also a public atmosphere favourably disposed towards negotiation and constructive management of conflict.

This academic task has, over many years, been closely matched with strong community and religious activities. I have represented the Religious Society of Friends (Quakers) of South and Southern Africa on several occasions, and have been involved in various programmes and conferences of the South African Council of Churches, the South African Institute of Race Relations, in protest groups concerning squatters, and so on. A Conflict Management Programme was launched in 1981 under joint auspices of the Centre for Intergroup Studies and the Western Province Council of Churches.

These activities inevitably give rise to my issuing public statements either in my private capacity or on behalf of one or more religious or community groups. Mass media seldom distinguish clearly between various platforms from which public statements are made. Reporters often merge (and even confuse) the roles of academic, community leader, or private individual. This conflict is manifested in several ways.

The public opinion-maker is seen as someone making a contribution to public thinking and political action. To the extent that he is successful and has an impact on constructive developments, he may claim and deserve credit. Such credit may, however, hamper progress if the facilitator instead of the contending parties is given credit for progress in negotiations. Facilitators should generally stay out of the public eye.

In private communication between parties the results and impact of errors in judgement, wrong choice of words, and wrong interpretations remain confined to the parties directly involved and can be rectified within that confined group. Public statements, however, have widespread impact. If repercussions are negative it is very difficult to rectify mistakes. Also, working through mass media enables other groups with vested interests to colour or slant interpretations and statements.

During 1986 I was involved in facilitating communication between Inkatha and the United Democratic Front (UDF) in Natal. There was good progress and both parties accepted my interpretation of the situation. During that time I wrote an article at the request of the *Sunday Times* on the current situation in South Africa with reference to the visit of the Eminent Persons Group (EPG) (van der Merwe 1986a). A week later Dr Mangosuthu G. Buthelezi, President of Inkatha, objected strongly to being 'singled out' in the article as 'the aggressive party' in South African politics. In a long letter to me he said I had become a propagandist for the UDF and had failed to remain neutral.

Two things had gone wrong. The *Sunday times*, either deliberately or because of shortage of space, had omitted a sentence in which special tribute was paid to Buthelezi as somebody willing to negotiate and compromise. The second mistake was my own poor choice of words. In the article I referred to 'the growing antagonism of Buthelezi towards the UDF and ANC' instead of the 'growing antagonism between Buthelezi and the UDF and the ANC'.

My explanation and apologies were accepted and I was able to continue my role as neutral facilitator. But this public incident could have ruined the private task. This in fact happened in the beginning of 1988 when the Chamber of Commerce in Natal had to withdraw their very able mediator, Mr Paul van Uytrecht, because a statement of his, published in the *New York Times*, offended Chief Buthelezi.

As an academic I became used to the slogan 'Publish or perish'. But, as a mediator, 'Publish and be damned!' might be more apt.

Another personal example illustrates the advantages of publicity. In December 1984 I introduced Dr Piet Muller, Assistant Editor of *Beeld*, the largest pro-Government Afrikaans daily paper, to members of the ANC executive committee in Lusaka. Requests for a meeting were made to me independently by the two parties. Dr Muller subsequently wrote two articles (*Beeld*, 12 and 13 December) in which he described common ground between the National Party and the African National Congress and, in an editorial, *Beeld* called on the Government to talk to the ANC.

This was the first contact of its kind in 24 years. Because of *Beeld*'s positive, constructive interpretation of an organization hitherto described only in antagonistic terms in pro-Government papers, the incident and his reports received world-wide publicity. *Beeld* mentioned that I had arranged this unique meeting. This led to speculation by newspapermen and others about my auspices and motives. There was even speculation that I was sent out as a feeler by the Government to test the ANC on the question of negotiation.

I decided it was necessary to make a public statement. I emphasized the independence of my position and mission and my positive approach and belief in the value of constructive steps towards communication between contending groups. These statements received considerable publicity in South Africa. Together with the positive stand of *Beeld*, they contributed towards public acceptance of the possibility of a negotiated settlement and growing public recognition of the ANC as a legitimate contending party within South Africa.

During the following two years more than two dozen delegations of white and black South African businessmen, academics, church leaders, and others met with the ANC in Lusaka. In a public opinion poll published by the Afrikaans Sunday paper *Rapport* by the middle of 1986 nearly 50 per cent of whites favoured talks with the Nationalist (as opposed to Communist) faction within the ANC (*Rapport*, 20 July 1986).

But the tension between my private and public activities continued over this period. Once I was approached by University of Stellenbosch student leaders to introduce them to the ANC youth league. This happened just two weeks after ANC leaders in Lusaka had asked for a meeting with Afrikaans-speaking students. I agreed on two conditions: that the government be informed beforehand and that the news be kept out of the press until the visit had taken place. *Die Burger*, a Nationalist newspaper, however, published a front page report that university student leadership accompanied by their Dutch Reformed Church chaplain planned to visit the ANC. The State President, who is Chancellor of the university, was embarrassed. The Minister of Home Affairs promptly confiscated the students' and the chaplain's passports.

The students who did *not* meet the ANC caused as much national and international publicity as the journalist who did. The Sunday paper *Rapport* devoted considerable space to sympathetic profiles of the students and the chaplain and summarized editorial comment by a number of pro-Government daily papers, all of which deplored the removal of their passports. An independent publisher, Taurus, commissioned a book on the incident which was published under the title *Praat met die ANC* (Talk to the ANC), written by Gerrit Olivier (1985).

While I am sorry this opportunity for dialogue was lost, it is my considered opinion that the public benefits of all this favourable publicity far outweighed the possible advantages these young people may have gained from the proposed visit. It is unlikely that they would have got as much publicity if they had indeed met. In fact, many of them did eventually meet with the ANC on later occasions.

Professional mediation service

In polarized situations opposing and conflicting groups do not communicate with each other. Peace initiatives and movements involved in mediation can play an important role in promoting meaningful communication. But polarization usually has the effect of eliminating the middle ground so that mediators, bridge-builders, and peacemakers are suspect on both sides.

The extent to which this has happened in South Africa is evident from the almost total absence of neutral mediating groups, peace initiatives, or movements in South Africa. While there are well over two hundred organizations and institutes in the United States of America exclusively concerned with the broad field of conflict resolution, there are virtually none in South Africa, other than those in industrial relations. Mediation, conciliation, and third-party intervention have been well developed in Europe and the United States, where such techniques are used to resolve community and national disputes. Independent third-party mediators and interveners are readily made available by a wide range of training programmes existing to develop relevant skills.

The South African situation differs in at least three respects. First, there are no formal organizations or initiatives, apart from the Centre for Intergroup Studies, which specifically offers training in communication skills for mediators or third-party interveners in community and political conflict. Second, the few mediating groups and peace initiatives which do exist originated in one or other interest group with a particular stand, so that few of them are quite neutral. Third, few organizations or initiatives outside industrial relations are primarily concerned with resolution of conflict (Winkler, van der Merwe, and Geldenhuys 1987).

Because of the intensity of (and South Africa's involvement in) the international debate about apartheid, few leading international political figures would be seen as sufficiently neutral on South African issues to be trusted by all major conflicting parties. I maintain, nevertheless, that the required qualities of neutrality and expertise can be found in several individuals, though not always combined in the same person. Our first task is to identify these people. There is a demand for an esteemed professional organization able to provide facilities where people with sufficient objectivity can be trained in conflict management skills. And such an organization could provide a home and moral base for this much-maligned middle group of people who can help to bridge the gap caused by polarization.

Modern insights and techniques have been applied successfully by the Independent Mediation Service of South Africa (IMSSA) and several other institutions in industrial relations in recent years, and by the South African Media Council in disputes involving the public media. The time is overdue for the establishment of a national mediation service specifically geared to serve in the fields of community and political conflict. IMSSA and overseas organizations could serve as models. Such a body could identify and train individuals to serve on a panel whose members could be called in by disputing parties to mediate.

Such a mediation service should be highly professional, but should not be divorced from or imposed on the people. Professionalization should entail training community and political leaders who are recruited from the community itself (van der Merwe 1986c). Many religious leaders, academics, and businessmen attempt mediation. I have referred earlier to some of their efforts. A national mediation service would serve to professionalize their services and make them more efficient. Costs of such services would probably be comparatively low as many religious and community leaders and academics serving on such panels would be willing to mediate for a small fee or without charging any fee.

Conclusion

While I have made a strong case for facilitation rather than mediation at times of extreme polarization (such as we have in South Africa at present), I have demonstrated from my own experience how facilitation has paved the way for mediation, and how I have responded.

This chapter reflects my current leanings towards the neutral role of facilitator or mediator in response to the acute need for more meaningful communication. I do, however, appreciate the need for pressures on the establishment, and argue that mediation and negotiation should be seen as *complementary* to, and not a substitute for, pressure. In Chapter 5 I argued that pressures should be constructive, conditional, and selective if they are to complement negotiation.

As a Quaker I am committed to non-violence. I have come to realize, however, that violence is endemic in mankind and in South Africa. Resort to violence is justified by virtually all religious and political leaders in all major conflicting groups in South Africa. I do believe, however, that the constructive approach described in this chapter will contribute towards a reduction of violence during the change process.

My efforts are directed towards promoting justice and peace in my country. These two goals are, however, unattainable ideals. Any new government in South Africa will fall short of these ideals. The struggle for justice, accompanied by violence, will continue, and so will the need for intermediaries.

Chapter seven

Prospects for the Constructive Accommodation of Conflict

While there is no Utopia in which full justice and stable peace can be achieved, I believe that the constructive accommodation of conflict in South Africa is indeed much more likely than is generally thought.

I have reviewed the wide range of current manifestations of conflict in South Africa, which clearly demonstrate its multi-dimensional nature, and have warned against oversimplification — the constant failing of politicians, demagogues, and ideologues.

In Chapter 4 I analyzed basic sources of conflict and came to the conclusion that a shift in fundamental ideologies has led to new political divisions and alliances. Apartheid ideology has found a new home in the Conservative Party, and the National Party is increasingly more motivated by pragmatic considerations and by a renewed commitment to a market-oriented socio-economic system. Consequently, the establishment is being broadened to include allies, who are not white, willing to operate within the capitalist system. The fundamental political division in the country is no longer traditional apartheid between white and black, but between the emerging market-oriented establishment and the extra-systemic opposition.

Because conflict has been so consistently badly handled it has become destructive and has led to the current state of polarization. But I have suggested that third-party intervention could make a major contribution towards better communication and the constructive accommodation of conflict. In this final chapter I assess some trends and consider prospects for such constructive accommodation.

Ideological commitment and pragmatic flexibility

As noted earlier, traditional apartheid ideology is making way for more pragmatic considerations in the current leadership of the National Party. This does not mean that there are no ideological commitments. There are, in fact, strong anti-communist, anti-socialist, and pro-free enterprise ideologies present in government circles, more particularly in the military establishment and certain business groups.

As the government abandons apartheid ideology, adherents of this ideology switch to the Conservative Party. Whether the Conservative Party will gain sufficient white electoral support to unseat the Nationalist government in the near future, is a matter of intense speculation. Traditional apartheid ideology undoubtedly still has strong support among the white masses.

How conservative or right-wing is the National Party? Ascertaining prevailing sentiments is difficult because of the deep internal divisions and the failure of National Party leadership to formulate clear goals for the future. White South African voters reflect this lack of direction. The unexpected swing to the National Party in the white election of May 1987 gave rise to world-wide assumptions of a 'rightward surge'. Allister Sparks described it as whites sealing their fate and many observers saw it as a 'last ditch' stand by whites. These observations are misplaced. As I understand current leadership in the National Party, their election manifesto, and the way they interpreted the election results and mandate of the voters, the result was not seen as a mandate to reinforce race discrimination.

The 1987 election was seen by the *verligtes* in the government as a mandate to continue with the reforms commenced after the 1977 election victory. Since then some 100 discriminatory laws have been abolished or adapted. These reforms include the abolition of racial discrimination in labour relations; integration in sport; admission of blacks to formerly 'white' universities; mixed business districts; repeal of the prohibition of mixed marriages and of sexual intercourse across the colour bar; repeal of the prohibition against mixed political parties; granting freedom of movement to all population groups by setting aside thirty-two individual enactments; complete elimination of statutory racial barriers in hotels and restaurants; and accessibility of blacks to most publicly-controlled recreational facilities (including beaches) (Thomashausen 1987: 14-18).

No National Party leaders called for the reinstatement of any of these racial restrictions or for a return to traditional apartheid.

If a vote for the National Party was not primarily a vote for apartheid then what was it for? I interpret the surge of votes for the National Party as a vote for security, but security interpreted in new ways. It was essentially for security amid reform. Most of those who voted for the National Party have accepted, at least intellectually, that apartheid must go. They know white rule is coming to an end. Their greatest fear now is *not* a black majority, but anxiety about the *process* through which black majority government will be achieved and how it will be manifested. In this situation the National Party offered more security than the small liberal splinter parties. These parties preached reform but could neither implement it nor promise security, because they would not be in positions of power to control the reform process they were advocating.

Those voters who wanted full apartheid restored voted for the Herstigte Nasionale Party (HNP) and the Conservative Party (CP), not the National Party. The Conservative Party offered to stop integration and promised to re-introduce influx control and apartheid in most of the areas where it had been abolished.

The swing of progressive-minded voters from the PFP to the NP should therefore not be interpreted as their having become more conservative. They believed that the party was *willing and able* to implement reform. This is clearly the way almost all top Nationalist leaders interpreted the results. For years observers have argued that the National Party has gradually been taking over PFP policies. A large number of former PFP voters appear to have adopted this point of view in the 1987 elections.

The Nationalist government, like any government, obviously wants to retain control. But desire to control or govern is motivated by some greater goal or purpose. For those leaders who now prevail in the National Party, including the State President and *verligte* members in the Cabinet and Parliament, this *ultimate* goal is not protection of white skins or white identity, nor even white rule, but protection of 'civilized standards', usually referred to as European or Western, and sometimes as white. Almost invariably the market-oriented economy or free enterprise is seen as the appropriate system and means for maintaining these standards.

To the extent that ideologies develop around socio-economic systems, ideological commitment is therefore present. But much of this ideological orientation is born out of fear of those hostile ideologies that threaten the 'system'. The 'total strategy' was developed as a response to the perceived total onslaught. The ideology of free enterprise lacks positive content. That is why I emphasize the importance of pragmatic considerations in current Nationalist leadership. This pragmatism introduces an element of flexibility which was lacking in the apartheid heyday.

Reorientation within Afrikaner religious and ethical beliefs and increasing flexibility in government thinking puts political protest into new perspective. It is seldom acknowledged publicly that the government admits that the present system is unjust and should be changed. During the campaign for the referendum on the new constitution in 1983, the State President repeatedly stated on public platforms that a new constitution was needed because the old constitution, which excluded coloured people and Indians from central government, was unjust. While Africans were excluded at that time, this was always understood to be a temporary exclusion.

The government does not spell out as clearly as in the 1983 campaign that the present system is unjust. But high-handed attempts to accommodate Africans in local, regional, and central government are clearly an attempt to gain legitimacy. In a major Budget Vote speech on 21 April 1988, the State president, P.W. Botha, re-committed himself to accommodate Africans on all levels of government. He proposed far-reaching changes to South Africa's political systems arguing that black communities outside the self-governing territories increasingly demand structures that would afford their participation in the governing process.

Related to the issue of justice are the issues of representativeness and legitimacy. The current three-chamber Parliament, though it includes coloured people and Indians, is still a minority government. The majority is *not* represented. For those with an apartheid mentality, this presents no problem because legitimacy is not seen to be based on democratic representation. But for those who are moving away from the apartheid mentality and whose political morality is becoming reshaped by Western political norms, this lack of representativeness has become a source of concern and embarrassment.

Why is the government so determined to move ahead with constitutional reform and the co-option of Africans into local regional and national government? While this is obviously motivated by a wish to extend its power base, I have no doubt it is also strongly motivated by deeper needs to establish legitimacy.

Majority rule and white security

It is not generally appreciated among opposition groups that the government, in spite of public denials, is implementing steps that will make majority rule inevitable (i.e. a system in which whites will be a numerical minority). This explains why so much emphasis is being placed on minority rights and white security. Were there to be white majority or white control, there would not be such concern about white minority rights and talk about the need for a white veto.

It was possible to incorporate the coloured people and Indians in the 1983 Constitution without having to face the problem of numbers. The fundamental ratio of four whites, two coloured people and one Indian was roughly representative of those population groups and still assured a white majority. But the incorporation of Africans could not be postponed indefinitely. The legitimate claim of Africans to be represented in central government has been appreciated on an intellectual level in Nationalist circles for a long time. Now that the time has arrived to implement this new insight the Nationalists are experiencing serious emotional obstacles. For a long time they have been trying to convince themselves that it would be possible to share power and still maintain white control. But in due course common sense is prevailing. There is no way in which Africans can be drawn into the current constitutional equation of four whites and three non-whites without the whites being outnumbered.

The burning question among Nationalists today is *not how to avoid majority rule*, but how to *protect white minority rights* in a majority system.

Admissions that the government lacks legitimacy inevitably grant a measure of legitimacy to the protest movement. This has several implications which can be constructively exploited. The government still refuses to admit that Nelson Mandela is a political prisoner. It is argued that he was sentenced for the ordinary crimes of planning violence, including violent overthrow of the government. Mandela has been explicit in his own defence and took pains to prove that (a) he had not resorted to indiscriminate violence but to a well-planned and rational armed struggle, and (b) that he decided on the armed struggle only as a *last resort* after all other avenues had been closed. This interpretation of the position of the ANC is today widely accepted, especially in church circles, and is appreciated even in the Dutch Reformed Church as being consistent with the theology of a just war. In radical circles it is also approved as being consistent with the theology of a just revolution.

While the government obviously cannot agree publicly to the legitimacy of any armed struggle or any theology of a just revolution, there is, in government circles today, some understanding of and sympathy for the position of a man like Mandela for whom all doors had indeed been closed in the 1960s when he resorted to the armed struggle. These new insights and new political and constitutional policies open up significant possibilities for the release of Mandela and other political prisoners.

The South African government is widely regarded as illegitimate because it does not represent the masses. As it expands its constituency by changing the constitution, first to include coloured people and Indians and, in the near future, Africans, it hopes to establish greater legitimacy. While radical movements will not publicly grant the government any legitimacy they are well aware of its changing policy and are willing to respond to it. More moderate leaders such as Buthelezi are publicly willing to co-operate, provided the pace of change is accelerated.

Although the government is not seen as legitimate it is recognized as a party to be dealt with. In the case of Inkatha, this recognition allows for direct dealing and negotiation. Ths implies recognition of the government as the *de jure*, if not legitimate, ruling power. For the ANC, such recognition, and direct dealing is less likely. It is probable that a third party, possibly a consortium of representatives of outside governments, would be required to mediate. Dr Stanley Mogoba, Secretary of the Methodist Church and President of the South African Institute of Race Relations, has made a convincing case for a renewed effort by such a mediating body.

Reconciling incremental steps with radical goals

Conflict and violence may be most intense when based on disagreement over means rather than goals. When disagreement over means occurs among those who share similar goals, severe conflict is generated because each faction sees the others as traitors to the cause. There is a natural tendency to accept that those who work for goals different from your own are your opponents or enemies. But if those who share your goals resort to means that appear contrary to your strategy and, especially, appear to threaten the hegemony and eventual success of your group, you will see them as traitors. This gives rise to an intense animosity that may surpass the hatred felt towards the common enemy and frequently leads to the splitting of protest or liberation groups.

The deepening of the division between those opposition groups willing to work within the prevailing socio-economic system (intra-systemic opposition) and those unwilling to do so (extra-systemic opposition) was described in Chapter 4. The intra-systemic group is willing to accept incremental steps towards fundamental change in South Africa. This strategy is seen by radical hard-liners as compromising, selling out, or being co-opted by the government. In the final analysis it is seen as supporting the system, strengthening the government and reinforcing apartheid, and therefore postponing the revolution and fundamental change.

Those refusing to participate in incremental steps demand fundamental structural change (i.e. the transfer of state power to the majority) as a condition for participation in institutional politics. Such structural change can, however, only come about through coercion, leaving no room for negotiation. These two conflicting approaches are clearly exemplified by two major opposition groups in South Africa, Inkatha and the UDF. Their fundamental ideological and political differences were discussed in Chapter 4. Here I merely underline their different strategies, namely whether or not opposition groups should participate in incremental steps towards fundamental change in the political system.

Inkatha is only one of the major groups which accepts incremental steps towards radical goals. There is also a developing multi-racial movement, with growing white participation and leadership, notably the new and independent candidates in Parliament and many church and community leaders. Many whites, including Afrikaners and nationalists, have come to accept the inevitability of fundamental political change. What they fear most is not radical change but uncontrolled and chaotic change. They seek some assurance that orderly change will be carried out by incremental steps.

These two major approaches need not be mutually exclusive. There is no reason why incremental steps cannot be reconciled with radical goals. Such steps should be clearly set out within an unequivocal programme for fundamental change. The demands for radical change should not be contrary to a rational plan of action. Making provision for a logical sequence of events is more likely to achieve the desired goal than planning a cataclysmic outburst.

Disagreement about the pace or rate of change is natural. Most whites who *do* realise that fundamental change, power-sharing and loss of privileges are inevitable, will instinctively do whatever is within their power to slow down this transition and will, therefore, propagate incremental change. Those who want to hasten that transition will favour quick change. This disagreement is on *means* and pace of change and not on eventual *goals*. While differences over means constitute severe causes of conflict, they are often more amenable to rational debate than differences over goals. Both parties presumably favour orderly change. The formulation of reasonable compromises should not be impossible. There are greater prospects for constructive accommodation of conflict than where there is ideological conflict.

Lewis Coser (1967: 28) makes a clear distinction between the processes of change within a system and the processes of change of a system. The change of a system is the drastic alteration of all major structural relations, its basic institutions and its prevailing value system. Change within a system and change of a system are not analytically divisible in practice, though a 'change of a system may be the result (or the sum total) of previous changes within the system' (Coser 1967: 28). Institutions may thus change gradually and nevertheless undergo basic transformation in their structural relations. The process of change is largely dependent on reaction to conflict by the system in power. 'Whether given forms of conflict will lead to changes in the social system or to breakdown and to formation of a new system will depend on the rigidity and resistance to change' (Coser 1967: 29).

I argue that there is indeed considerable flexibility in the present establishment and a genuine willingness to tolerate change. This approach has allowed a wide range of minor reforms which have been dismissed by cynics as 'cosmetic change'. It is not appreciated by these critics that an accumulation of minor 'cosmetic' changes eventually adds up to fundamental structural change.

While the government intends to allow only limited and tightly controlled change, opposition groups have managed to wrest some control of the process from the reformers. Minor reforms have opened avenues of influence to a range of pressure groups that now have some access to state decision-making.

The strategy of co-option has undeniably undermined some opposition leaders willing to work within the system, accepting incremental change. Many of them have been successfully neutralized and constitute little or no threat to the system. But the political participation of some of these people has led to development of new relationships and new social forces that cannot be contained within the old system of apartheid. The system is being transformed in the direction of fundamental structural change.

Progressive trade unions have found that participation in legal structures under government auspices has provided organizational and legal space for the consolidation of their power. Such participation provided growth and empowerment for Fosatu (the Federation of South African Trade Unions). While there was initially considerable ambivalence about the advisability of obtaining government recognition, in practice it provided African unions with valuable opportunities. Participation in state structures and negotiation with the government undoubtedly served as means of empowerment. The remarkable success of trade union negotiations had an impact on progressive mass-based political groups, especially those affiliated to the UDF.

During 1987 there were many negotiations between the two major contesting groups — establishment and extra-systemic opposition — in various cities, towns, and communities. These local-level negotiations have brought home to extra-systemic opposition groups the importance of short-term gains and realizable goals. Short-term gains consolidate strength for attaining long-term goals. Political groups gradually realized that, as with trade unions, they need not compromise fundamental goals and principles by participating in some aspects of the existing system.

While it was true that participation in the system conferred some legitimacy on the government it was also true that practical participation, rather than radical rhetoric, conferred legitimacy on their own organizations in the eyes of the masses. The increasingly strong powerbase of protest groups in the late 1980s reduced the dangers of co-option by the state and therefore participation and negotiation have become more viable options. Radical groups can now move beyond purely reactive boycott tactics and can shed the boycott mentality.

Legitimation and institutionalization of alternative social structures

The development of alternative social and political structures and their institutionalization is an inevitable component of the democratization process in South Africa. These developments carry with them a shift of legitimacy from conventional governmental systems to alternative structures and they constitute a major threat to the government.

Alternative structures developed in industrial relations largely to meet two major needs, representation and conflict management. African trade unions developed in spite of government resistance and its refusal to recognize them. A logical consequence of their development was the need for institutions to regulate conflict between labour and management. Because the state failed to provide for these needs, alternative structures developed to meet the needs of the society, and more specifically those of labour and management. Initially they were illegal, but because they were representative, they were recognized as legitimate by the people. Because they worked they were used by management. In the post-Wiehahn period they have become legally institutionalized. The growth of extra-systemic opposition, described in Chapter 4, has created a similar potential for development of alternative social and political structures. Opposition groups have operated outside the system partly because they were excluded by the establishment and partly because they refused to operate within the system. Their refusal was partly for tactical reasons — the fear of being co-opted, or of conferring legitimacy on the government — but was often motivated by what I have called the boycott mentality.

Awareness of political strength, power, and confidence has enabled them to reconsider strategy. There is now less fear of being co-opted. They have learned lessons in industrial relations: legal recognition can provide organizational space for empowerment and bargaining. Industrial relations offer good examples of how the old bureaucracy failed to accommodate new developments. Extra-statutory procedures and systems began to develop to meet contemporary needs. Traditional institutions such as liaison and work committees failed to meet actual needs largely because they were imposed by the authorities and were not representative. Management started to negotiate with unregistered African unions instead. The investment by the state of liaison and work committees with authority, could not grant them legitimacy. Increasing extra-statutory communication, whether bargaining or negotiation, led to institutionalization of newly developed legitimate, though not legal, systems.

Legitimized control 'refers to authority that is derived from those over whom it is exercised' (Burton 1979: 130). The increase in extra-statutory negotiations that took place prior to Wiehahn in industry and current negotiations taking place in community and constitutional affairs, reflect the demand for negotiating bodies which are perceived as legitimate by the constituencies. In other words, successful negotiation can only occur between legitimate leaders. Empowerment and legitimacy are two integrally related concepts. Power requires legitimacy. 'Power springs up whenever people get together and act in concert, but it derives its legitimacy from the initial getting together rather than from any action that then may follow' (Arendt 1970: 52). Neither trade unions nor any other organizations can be empowered simply by the state investing them with authority.

The Wiehahn reforms institutionalized certain extra-statutory procedures which were already functioning successfully and were seen as legitimate. Following this pattern the state, in its long-term interests, will have to allow extra-parliamentary and extra-statutory opposition groups legal space to become democratic, representative and therefore legitimate organizations of the majority of South Africans with ability to negotiate on their behalf.

Experience in industrial relations in South Africa has also demonstrated how important it is that conflict management is institutionalized. The Wiehahn Commission prepared the framework for real negotiations to take place because, for the first time, African trade unions were recognized as legitimate and representative bargaining partners. This principle must now be addressed in constitutional and political affairs.

In industrial relations we now have a clearly demarcated grievance procedure, the legal recognition of legitimate contending parties and the identification and recognition of third parties. Within this conflict resolution structure there is a clearly defined role for a third party (mediator/ arbitrator), and a definition of the stages at which these bodies may be introduced. The question of formal negotiating procedures now needs to be addressed in political conflict management where the state has not yet begun to recognize the legitimacy of alternative structures which have managed conflict successfully. A rare but welcome exception was a statement by the Minister of Development and Training, acknowledging the value of 'peoples' education'!

Current emergency regulations, however, seem designed to oppress not only development of representative and legitimate extra-systemic opposition groups, but also any successful mechanism to regulate conflict between these groups and progovernment bodies. During 1987 there was a significant increase in local level negotiations across the major divide between establishment and extra-systemic groups.

Many representatives of broad-based extra-systemic opposition groups such as the UDF, the National Education Crisis Committee (NECC), and the Soweto Parents Crisis Committee (SPCC), conducted negotiations with business leaders, representing organizations such as the Chamber of Commerce, with political leaders from parliamentary parties, with white local government officials and civil servants, and often with the security forces themselves. In Natal, negotiations between the UDF and Inkatha got under way. Almost invariably, apparently on instructions from security heads in Pretoria, spokesmen for progressive organizations were detained, often when negotiations were becoming successful.

It seems that these organizations are seen as a comparatively greater threat to the establishment once they engage *successfully* in extra-statutory mechanisms to control and manage conflict. These negotiations took place among autonomous bodies outside state sanction at a time when the government was repeatedly making futile attempts to draw extra-parliamentary opposition groups into its own constitutional proposal. The state seemed unable to accept that these negotiations reflected social reality, that these negotiating bodies should be sanctioned, and that attempts should be made to accommodate them in open discussions in the new constitutional dispensation.

There are several understandable reasons why the government is failing at this stage to implement lessons it should have learned from its experience with industrial relations. Ideological commitment produces closed minds. The perception of the total onslaught does not allow for constructive accommodation of conflict or for negotiated settlements. Another major difficulty is found in the organizational and structural contrast between the political opposition groups and trade unions. The unions were the properly constituted organizational representatives of their constituencies, but progressive community organizations do not represent any properly constituted political party or group. The major political parties had been banned. The UDF is a loose federation of several hundred community organizations and churches. To identify representative leaders with clear mandates is often a problem, especially as recognized leaders are often detained. Apart from Inkatha and the parliamentary coloured and Indian parties there are, at present, no clearly formulated opposition policies, strategies, or hierarchies and discipline, and in many communities there is anarchy.

The pursuit of justice and peace

The goals of social justice (equality and human rights) and peace (conciliation) are complementary: you cannot have one without the other. Neither can therefore be pursued exclusively. It follows that the means used to pursue these two goals are also complementary. I suggested empowerment and conciliation as two broad areas of constructive intervention in the pursuit of these goals.

Although I have used the term 'empowerment' which has ultimate political connotations, I have given it a broad base which includes development, education, training, and confidence-building. Power is an essential component of the political process. It is the mechanism used to coerce opponents towards acceptable behaviour or away from unacceptable behaviour. In this sense it is a major means for pursuing justice. Negotiation is a major means of achieving conciliation between contending parties.

Coercion and negotiation seem at first glance to be mutually exclusive. I have argued that they are complementary and that coercion is part of the negotiation process in political relations. Without coercion, negotiation deteriorates into cheap conciliation; without negotiation, coercion becomes merely punitive and destructive.

Empowerment of black communities through mobilization and establishment of legitimate alternative economic, political, and social structures, and with concurrent weakening of illegitimate government institutions, will contribute towards greater symmetry of power. This will enhance the prospects of negotiated settlement.

While the two goals of justice and peace are complementary, they also stand in a relationship of tension towards each other. This tension is especially manifested in the differing roles of peacemaker (conciliator) and prophet (proponent of justice). The peacemaker or conciliator must have credibility on both sides of a conflict. Maintaining good relationships and credibility with all parties is not compatible with the angry prophet's exposure of, or attacks on, injustice, or with public confrontation of the perceived perpetrators of injustice. The responsibilities, tasks, and styles of peacemakers and prophets are different, and can cause severe tensions within any one person or between persons and groups.

In the same sense that peace and justice as goals are complementary, peacemaking and the promotion of justice as means towards these goals are also complementary; one should not be conducted without the other. An obsession with the promotion of justice at all costs, will undermine the foundations of peace and of a stable lasting future society. There will always be tension between the deprived who will be preoccupied with the pursuit of justice — sometimes obsessively — and the privileged, who will attempt to retain apparent peace in order not to disturb the *status quo*.

The goals of absolute justice and stable peace are ultimately unattainable. The term 'conflict *resolution*' does not apply to fundamental social problems in South Africa. Underlying causes of conflict cannot be completely removed. This is apparent from the review of manifestations of conflict in Chapter 3 and the discussion of underlying causes of conflict in Chapter 4. Resolution could be interpreted as 'cheap conciliation' (i.e. conciliation without the removal of fundamental injustices). For that reason this book has been concerned with the constructive accommodation of conflict in South Africa.

Since gross inequalities and injustices are built into social and political institutions in South Africa, fundamental structural change is essential for constructive accommodation of conflict. Without radical change, justice and peace cannot be successfully pursued.

Meaningful change will require new political institutions for all levels of government, in which all population groups, regardless of race or ethnicity, would have direct representation. In Western democratic terms it would mean majority rule. Of course, neither fundamental structural change nor majority rule can guarantee justice and peace. Material inequality and injustices as well as ideological differences will persist albeit in new forms and manifestations.

Our present task is to work towards constructive accommodation of conflict in our continuing pursuit of justice and peace. I have argued that this is indeed much more likely than popularly perceived.

Bibliography

Albert, Jean (1986) *Negotiation Skills: A Handbook*, Cape Town: Centre for Intergroup Studies (Conflict and Peace Studies Series no. 2).
Arendt, Hannah (1970) *On Violence*. London: Allen Lanes, The Penguin Press.
Bailey, Sydney D. (1985) 'Non-official mediation in disputes: reflections on Quaker experience', *International Affairs*: 205-22.
Banks, Michael (1987) 'Conflict resolution'. Unpublished paper.
Barratt, John (1988) *South Africa and Its Neighbours: Co-operation or Conflict?* Johannesburg: South African Institute of International Affairs (Occasional Paper).
Bercovitch, J. (1984) *Social Conflicts and Third Parties: Strategies of Conflict Resolution*, Boulder, Colorado: Westview Press.
Berman, Maureen R. and Joseph E. Johnson (eds) (1977) *Unofficial Diplomats*, New York: Columbia.
Boulding, Kenneth (1978) *Stable Peace*, Austin, Texas: University of Texas.
Braun, Gerald and Heribert Weiland (1987) 'Sanctions against South Africa — too few, too late', paper presented at the Workshop on Change in South Africa at the Annual Conference of the European Consortium for Political Research, Amsterdam, 11-15 April.
Burton, J.W. (1968) *System, State, Diplomacy and Rules*, London: Cambridge University Press.
—— (1979) *Deviance, Terrorism and War*, Oxford: Martin Robertson.
Clark, J. (1983) 'Towards a sociology of labour law', in Wedderburn *et al.* (eds), *Labour Law and Industrial Relations: Building on Kahn-Freund* (pp. 81-106), Oxford: Clarendon Press.
Coser, Lewis A. (1967) *Continuities in the Study of Social Conflict*, New York: The Free Press.
Curle, Adam (1981) *True Justice: Quaker Peace Makers and Peace Making*, Swarthmore Lecture, London: Quaker Home Service.
—— (1986) *In the Middle: Non-official Mediation in Violent Situations*, Leamington Spa: Berg (Bradford Peace Studies NS, 1).
Degenaar, J. (1987) 'The politics of negotiation: politics is an interplay of pressures', South African Institute of Race Relations (Regional Topic Paper: 87/7).
De Klerk, W.A. (1975) *The Puritans in Africa: A Story of Afrikanerdom*, London: Rex Collings.

Bibliography

De Kock, Wessel (1986) *Usuthu! Cry Peace!: The Black Liberation Movement Inkatha and the Fight for a Just South Africa*, Cape Town: The Open Hand Press.

Desmond, Cosmas (1978) *Christians or Capitalists? Christianity and Politics in South Africa*, London: The Bowerdeen Press.

Deutsch, Morton (1973) *The Resolution of Conflict: Constructive and Destructive Processes*, New Haven, New Jersey: Yale University Press.

Dewar, D., A. Todes, and V. Watson (1982) *Theories of Urbanisation and National Settlement Strategy in South Africa*, Cape Town: University of Cape Town, Urban Problems Research Unit.

Eberstadt, Nicholas (1988) 'Poverty in South Africa', *Optima* 36 (March): 20–33.

Falk, Richard A., and Samuel S. Kim (eds) (1980) *The War System: An interdisciplinary approach*, Boulder, Colorado: Westview Press.

Foster, Don (1987) *Detention and Torture in South Africa: Psychological, Legal and Historical Studies*, Cape Town: David Philip.

Glaser, Kurt and S.T. Possony (1979) *Victims of Politics: The State of Human Rights*, New York: Columbia University Press.

Greenberg, Stanley (1980) *Race and State in Capitalist Development: South Africa in Comparative Perspective*, Johannesburg: Ravan.

Gurr, Ted Robert (ed.) (1980) *Handbook on Political Conflict*, New York: The Free Press.

Hanf, T., H. Weiland, and G. Vierdag (1981) *South Africa: The Prospects of Peaceful Change*, London: Rex Collings; Cape Town: David Philip; Bloomington: Indiana University Press.

Haysom, Nicholas (1986) *Mabangala: The Rise of Right Wing Vigilantes in South Africa*, Johannesburg: University of the Witwatersrand, Centre for Applied Legal Studies.

Hund, John (ed.) (1988) *Law and Justice in South Africa*, Johannesburg: Institute for Public Interest Law and Research; Cape Town: Centre for Intergroup Studies.

Hund, John and Hendrik W. van der Merwe (1986) *Legal Ideology and Politics in South Africa: A Social Science Approach*, London: University Press of America; Cape Town: Centre for Intergroup Studies.

Kairos Theologians (1985) *The Kairos Document*, Braamfontein: Kairos Theologians.

Kaunda, Kenneth D. (1980) *Kaunda on Violence*, edited by Colin M. Morris, London: Collins.

Killick, John (1983) *The Total Onslaught: How Does it Look from Moscow?* Cape Town: South African Institute of International Affairs (Occasional Paper).

Leach, Graham (1986) *South Africa: No Easy Path to Peace*, London: Methuen.

Leatt, James, Theo Kneifel, and Klaus Nürnberger (1986) *Contending Ideologies in South Africa*, Grand Rapids: Wm. B. Eerdmans; Cape Town: David Philip.

Lenski, Gerhard E. (1966) *Power and Privilege*, New York: McGraw-Hill.

Lodge, T. (1983) *Black Politics in South Africa Since 1945*, Johannesburg: Ravan Press.

Meyer, Gabi, Hendrik W. van der Merwe, and Wanita Kawa (1986) *Conflict Accommodation: Towards Conceptual Clarification*, Cape Town: Centre for Intergroup Studies (Conflict and Peace Studies Series no. 1).

Bibliography

Meyer, Gabi, Hendrik W. van der Merwe, and Karen Honikman (1988) 'Peace initiatives in South Africa: problems and challenges', paper presented at the 38th Annual Conference of the International Communication Association, New Orleans, 29 May-2 June.
Moss, Glen (1980) 'Total strategy', *Work in Progress* 11 (February): 1-11.
Nel, Philip (1988) 'Does Moscow want South African minerals?' *Optima* 36, no. 1 (March): 34-41.
Nolutshungu, Sam C. (1983) *Changing South Africa: Political Considerations*, Cape Town: David Philip.
Olivier, Gerrit (ed.) (1985) *Praat met die ANC*, Pretoria: Taurus.
O'Meara, D. (1983) *Volkskapitalisme: Class, Capital and Ideology in the Development of Afrikaner Nationalism 1934-1948*, Cambridge: Cambridge University Press.
Orkin, Mark (1986) *Disinvestment, the Struggle and the Future: What Black South Africans Really Think*, Johannesburg: Ravan Press.
Rex, J. (1981) *Social Conflict: A Conceptual and Theoretical Analysis*, London: Longman.
Rhoodie, N.J. (1969) *Apartheid and Racial Partnership in Southern Africa*, Cape Town: Academica.
—— (1983) *Intergroup Conflict in Deeply Segmented Societies: An introductory conceptual framework*. Pretoria: Human Sciences Research Council.
Rhoodie, N.J. and H.J. Venter (1960) *Apartheid: A Socio-historical Exposition of the Origin and Development of the Apartheid Idea*, Amsterdam: De Bussy.
Runciman, W.G. (1968) 'Class, status and power', in J.A. Jackson (ed.) *Social Stratification* (pp. 25-61), Cambridge: Cambridge University Press.
Schermerhorn, R.A. (1970) *Comparative Ethnic Relations*, New York: Random House.
Slabbert, Frederick Van Zyl and David Welsh (1979) *South Africa's Options: Strategies for Sharing Power*, Cape Town: David Philip.
South Africa Bureau for Information (1987) *The National State of Emergency*, Pretoria: Bureau for Information.
South African Council of Churches (1983) *Conscientious Objection: A Counsellor's Resource Manual*, Johannesburg: South African Council of Churches.
South African Institute of Race Relations (SAIRR) (1985) *Survey of Race Relations in South Africa*, Johannesburg: South African Institute of Race Relations.
—— (1986) *Survey of Race Relations in South Africa*, Johannesburg: South African Institute of Race Relations.
Southern African Catholic Bishops' Conference (1985) *The Things That Make for Peace*, Pretoria: Southern African Catholic Bishops' Conference.
Stadler, Alf (1987) *The Political Economy of Modern South Africa*, Cape Town: David Philip; London: Croom Helm.
Sunter, Clem (1987) *The World and South Africa in the 1990s*, Cape Town: Human & Rousseau.
Teichman, Jenny (1986) *Pacifism and the Just War: A Study in Applied Philosophy*, Oxford: Blackwell.
Thomashausen, André E.A.M. (1987) *The Dismantling of Apartheid: The Balance*

of Reforms 1978-1988, Pretoria: Thomashausen.
Van den Berg, Owen and Brian O'Connell (1986) 'An unfinished school crisis in the Cape of Storms', *Indicator SA* (Autumn); 3-4.
Van den Berghe, Pierre L. (1965) *South Africa: A study in conflict*, Berkeley: University of California Press.
van der Merwe, Hendrik W. (1981) *South Africa: Morality and Action: Quaker Efforts in a Difficult Environment*. Chicago: Progresiv Publishr (Studies in Quakerism no. 7); Cape Town: Centre for Intergroup Studies (Occasional Paper no. 6).
—— (1982) 'Is there a shift from race to class conflict in South Africa?' in *South African Sociological Association Referate/Papers 1982* (pp. 323-8), Pretoria: SASA.
—— (1983a) 'Mediation and empowerment in South Africa', in A. Paul Hare (ed.) *The Struggle for Democracy in South Africa: Conflict and Conflict Resolution* (pp. 18-29), Cape Town: Centre for Intergroup Studies.
—— (1983b) 'Urbanisation and the political position of Africans in South Africa', *South African Journal of Sociology* 14, no. 4: 109-17.
—— (1986a) 'Like it or not, we may need third-party help', *Sunday Times*, 1 June 1986.
—— (1986b) 'Peace marshalling: a case study of social control,' paper presented at a working group on Conflict and Peace Studies at the Seventeenth Annual Congress of the Association for Sociology in Southern Africa, Durban, 30 June-4 July.
—— (1986c) 'Towards the professionalisation of Conflict and Peace Studies in South Africa', opening address of the First National Conference on Negotiation and Mediation in Community and Political Conflict, Durban, 4 July.
—— (1987) 'A plea for conscientious affirmation', *The Friend* 145 (April): 415-6.
(1988) 'South African initiatives: contrasting options in the mediation process', in Christopher Mitchell and Keith Webb (eds) *New Approaches to International Mediation*, Westport: Greenwood Press.
van der Merwe, Hendrik W., M.J. Ashley, Nancy C.J. Charton, and Bettina J. Huber (1974) *White South African Elites*, Cape Town: Juta.
van der Merwe, Hendrik W., and John Hendricks (1983) 'Manifestations of violence in the South African conflict', paper presented at the Workshop of the Centre for Intergroup Studies on Conflict and Conflict Accommodation in South Africa, Cape Town, August.
van der Merwe, Hendrik W., and David Welsh (eds) (1972) *Student Perspectives on South Africa*, London: Rex Collings; Cape Town: David Philip.
Villa-Vicencio, Charles (1977) 'South Africa's theologized nationalism', *The Ecumenical Review* 29 (October): 373-82.
Villa-Vicencio, Charles (ed.) (1987) *Theology and Violence: The South African Debate*, Johannesburg: Skotaville.
Webb, Keith and Hendrik W. van der Merwe (1987) 'Mapping complexity and a negotiated future in South Africa', paper presented at the Workshop on Change in South Africa at the Annual Conference of the European Consortium for Political Research, Amsterdam, 10-15 April.
Wink, Walter (1987) *Jesus' Third Way: The Relevance of Nonviolence in South Africa Today*, Johannesburg: South African Council of Churches.

Bibliography

Winkler, Renate, Hendrik W. van der Merwe, and Odette Geldenhuys (1987) *An Overview of Peace Initiatives, Movements and Organisations in South Africa*. Cape Town: Centre for Intergroup Studies (Conflict and Peace Studies Series no. 4).

Zille, Helen (1987) 'People's education — an opportunity lost', *Die Suid-Afrikaan* 9 (Lente/Somer): 25–8.

Index

affirmation, conscientious 75-6
African National Congress (ANC) 59; banned 30, 73; and communism 80; and constitution 28; Freedom Charter 60; and negotiation 102; and non-violence 73; and violence 32-4, 92, 109
Afrikaanse Protestante Kerk (APK) 43, 51
Albert, Jean 14-15, 164
alliances, political 58-60
apartheid 22-9; and capitalism 53-7; and churches 48-9, 51-2; Conservative Party 52, 105-6, 107; erosion of 49-51; grand 22-8; as ideological force 12-13; legislation 22, 24-5, 29-30; National Party 48, 52, 77; petty 28-9
Arendt, Hannah 113
assassinations 36
avoidance of conflict 63
Azanian Peoples' Organisation (Azapo) 36, 59

Bailey, Sydney D. 96
Banks, Michael 96
banning of organizations, *etc.* 29-30
Barratt, Prof. John 66-7, 79
Barth, Karl 57
Beeld 101-2
Bercovitch, J. 88
Berman, Maureen R. 91, 96
Black Alliance 27

Black Labour Relations Regulation Act (1953) 67
Black Sash 25
Boesak, Dr Allan 41, 51
Bophuthatswana 23
Botha, P.W. 56, 77, 78, 107-8
Botswana 84
Boulding, Kenneth 1
boycotts 73-4; consumer 38-9; education 37-8; elections 27; mentality 80-1; rent 25; *see also* sanctions
Braun, Gerald 81-2
Burton, John W. 77, 90, 97, 113
Buthelezi, Bishop Manas 41
Buthelezi, Dr Mangosuthu, Chief 27, 41, 101, 109

capitalism 11-12; and apartheid 53-7
Centre for Intergroup Studies 32
change 110-12, 116; rate of 110-11
Chikane, Revd Frank 41
churches: and apartheid 48-9, 51-2; and state 41-3; and violence 42, 61, 71
Ciskei 23
citizenship 24-5
civil disobedience 72, 74-6
'civilization' 20
class *see* social structure
coercion 65, 66, 115-16
cognitive dissonance theory 68
communication 7, 65, 67; improving 94-7
communism 77-80

Index

compromise 63
conciliation 7, 115-16
conflict 14-16, 62, 69; approaches to 61-86; dimensions of stratification 9-14; and ideology 46-8; and inequality 17, 19; manifest and latent 5-6
Congress of South African Trade Unions (Cosatu) 28, 36, 40-1, 59
conscientious affirmation 75-6
Conservative Party (CP) 26, 42, 49; and constitution 28; ideology 52, 105-6, 107; and power 76-7
constitution of South Africa 25-7, 108
constructive intervention 1-8, 62-5; prospects for 105-17
consultation 68
consumer boycotts 38-9
co-operation 66-7
co-option 67-8, 111-12
Coser, Lewis A. 111
Criminal Procedures Act 40
Curle, Adam xiii-xv, 91

Defiance of Unjust Laws Campaign 72
Degenaar, J. 66
De Klerk, W.A. 48-9
De Kock, Wessel 59
deprivation 19
Desmond, Cosmas 11, 57
Detainees' Parents' Support Committee (DPSC) 30
detentions 30, 40
Deutsch, Morton 98
development 6
Dewar, D. 24
disobedience, civil 72, 74-6
Doncaster, Shifa and Hugh 93
Duncan, Sheena 74
Dutch Reformed Churches (DRC) 12-13, 26, 42-3, 48-9, 51

Eberstadt, Nicholas 18
economic dimension of stratification 10-12
education, revolt 37-8

elections 27
emergency, state of 30, 31, 40
Eminent Persons Group (EPG) 99, 101
empowerment 6, 115-16
equality 49, 115-16; *see also* inequality

Falk, Richard A. 62
Federation of South African Trade Unions (Fosatu) 112
Festinger, Leon 68
force 17; *see also* violence
Foster, Don 30
fragmentation 5
Freedom Charter 60

Gandhi 72
Geldenhuys, Odette 41, 103
Gereformeerde Kerk 51
Glaser, Kurt 11
Goniwe, Mathew 36
government *see* National Party
Greenberg, Stanley 12
Groom, John 97
Group Areas Act (1950) 22, 29
Gumede, Archie 27
Gurr, Ted Robert 64, 94

Hanf, T. 10-14, 18
Haysom, Nicholas 35-6
Hendricks, John 32-4
Herstigte Nasionale Party 26, 28, 52, 107
Hervormde Kerk 51
Heyns, Prof. Johan 43
Hoivik, Tord 94
homelands policy 23
housing 23, 25
human rights 1, 115-16
Hund, John 58, 60

ideology: apartheid 12-13, 48-51; commitment to 76-81, 105-8; and conflict 46-8; homelands 23; inequality 20-1; Marxism 53, 56-7
Indaba 28, 59
Independent Mediation Service of

South Africa (IMSSA) 103-4
inequality 3, 4-5, 17-18, 49; and
  conflict 17, 19; ideology 20-1
injustice 3, 4-5; *see also* inequality
Inkatha 59; and constitution 27-8;
  and negotiation 109, 114; and
  trade unions 40-1; and UDF 36,
  60, 101, 110, 114
Internal Security Act 40
intervention constructive 1-8, 62-5;
  force 6, 87-104; need for 87-90;
  prospects for 105-17; *see also*
  mediation
Intimidation Act 40

Jack, Mkhuseli 39
Johnson, Joseph E. 91, 96
joint problem-solving 63
justice 1-4, 115-16

Kairos Document 17, 41-2, 71
Kaunda, Kenneth D. 16-17, 71, 84
Kgame, Steve 27
Khanyile, Vusi 38
Killick, John 57
Kim, Samuel S. 62
King, Coretta 89
King, Martin Luther 72
Kneifel, Theo 47
Kwazulu 23, 28, 59

Labour Party 27
labour relations 39-41
Land Act (1913) 24
Landman, Dr W.A. 51
Leach, Graham 58
Leatt, James 47
legislation, apartheid 22, 24-5,
  29-30
legitimacy 112-15
Lenski, Gerhard E. 10, 47
Lipset, S.M. 49-50
Lodge, Tom 44, 60
Lombard, Prof. Jan 55-6
Lusaka statement 42
Luthuli, Albert 72

McNamara, Robert S. 62
majority rule 108-15

Malan, General 78, 92
Mandela, Nelson 109
Mandela, Winnie 89
Mannheim, Karl 47
market economy 53-7
Marx, Karl 11
Marxism 53, 56-7
mediation 7, 88-104; concern 91-4;
  face-saving 98-104; identification
  of issues and needs 97-8;
  improving communication 94-7;
  neutrality 90; private and public
  roles 99-102; professional 103-4
militarization 30, 74
Mogoba, Dr Stanley 109
Moss, Glen 78
Mozambique 84
Muller, Dr Piet 101
Mxenge, Mrs Victoria 36

Natal 28, 36, 114
National Building Institute 25
National Council of Trade Unions
  (Nactu) 40
National Education Crisis
  Committee (NECC) 37-8, 114
National Forum Committee (NFC)
  38, 59
National Party (NP) 58, 77;
  apartheid ideology 48, 52, 77;
  apartheid measures 22-9; and
  capitalism 53-5; changes 52,
  105-8; and the church 42-3, 48;
  and constitution 25-8; homeland
  policy 23-4; pragmatism 52,
  105-8; urbanization 24-5
National Security Management
  System 30
National Statutory Council (NSC)
  27
Naude, Dr Beyers 41-2, 51
Ndondo, Balandwa 36
Nederduits Gereformeerde Kerk 51
Nederduits Gereformeerde
  Sendingkerk 51
negotiation 65-8, 70, 88, 115-16
Nel, Dr Philip 79-80
New Republican Party (NRP) 28
Nolutshungu, Sam C. 44, 54

Index

non-violence 71-4
Nürnberger, Klaus 47

O'Connell, Brian 38
Olivier, Gerrit 102
O'Meara, Dan 53
Orkin, Mark 82

Paisley, Revd Ian 87
Pan Africanist Congress (PAC) 30, 59, 73
passive resistance 72-4
Paton, Alan 77
peace 1-4, 115-16
pessimism 62
'plural society' 21
polarization 5, 69-70
political dimension of stratification 10-12
political rights 22-3, 108-15
politics, changes 58-60
population, black and white 17-18
Population Registration Act 22
Possony, S.T. 11
power 70-4, 113
press 101-2
Progressive Federal Party (PFP) 26-7, 59, 107
Prohibition of Illegal Squatting Act (1986) 24, 25
Prohibition of Mixed Marriages Act 22
Public Safety Act (1953) 29-30

Quakers 72, 75-6, 93, 100

race 50-1; discrimination *see* apartheid; and polarization 5
Repport 31, 102
Regional Services Councils 28
religion *see* churches
Religious Society of Friends (Quakers) 72, 75-6, 93, 100
relocation of Africans 23-4, 29
repression, political 29
resolution of conflict 6, 91, 116; obstacles to 68-70
Rex, J. 11
Rhoodie, Nic J. 19, 48

rights: human 1, 115-16; political 22-3, 108-15
Runciman, W.G. 13

sanctions, international 81-6
Schermerhorn, R.A. 12
Schlebusch Commission 26
Scholtz, G.D. 51
security, white 108
settlement 6
Sharpeville massacre 72-3
siege mentality 76-80
Slabbert, Frederick Van Zyl 54-5
smoothing conflict 63
social structure 7 alternatives 112-15; change 110-12, 116; stratification 9-12, 13-14, 20
socialism 55, 60
socio-cultural dimension of stratification 10-12
South African Broadcasting Corporation (SABC) 34, 55-6, 78
South Africa Bureau for Information 31, 35
South African Council of Churches (SACC) 41, 74, 75-6, 100
South African Defence Force (SADF) 30, 92
South African Institute of Race Relations (SAIRR) 4, 100; boycotts 38, 39; constitution 27; inequality 18; relocations 24; trade unions 41; violence 31-2, 35
South West African Peoples Organisation (Swapo) 42, 80
Southern African Catholic Bishops' Conference 1, 41
Soweto Parents Crisis Committee (SPCC) 37, 114
Soweto riots 26, 43
Sparks, Allister 106
Special Cabinet Committee (SCC) 27
special constables 36-7
squatting 24, 25
Stadler, Alf 43-4, 53
stratification, social 9-12, 13-14, 20

Index

strikes 39-41
Sunter, Clem 66

TBVC countries 23
Tambo, Oliver 31
Teichman, Jenny 16
Theron Commission 26
Thomashausen, André E.A.M. 106
Tocqueville 49
Todes, A. 24
torture 30
townships, violence 35-7
trade unions 40-1, 112-13
Transkei 23
transport, boycotts 39
Trespass Act 25
Treurnicht, Dr Andries 26, 49, 76
tri-cameral system 26-8
Tutu, Bishop Desmond 4, 41, 71, 72-3, 88

Union of Soviet Socialist Republics (USSR) 77-80
United Democratic Front (UDF) 26-7, 59, 115; and boycotts 38; and constitution 28; Freedom Charter 60; and Inkatha 36, 60, 101, 110, 114; and negotiation 114; and violence 36
United Kingdom (UK) 47, 82
United States of America (USA) 20-1, 47
United Workers Union of South Africa (Uwusa) 40-1, 59
Urban Councils Association of South Africa (UCASA) 27
urbanization 24-5

van den Berg, Owen 38

van den Berghe, Pierre L. 21
van der Merwe, Hendrik W. 4, 32-4, 41, 50, 58, 103-4
van Uytrecht, Paul 101
Venda 23
Venter, H.J. 48
verligtheid 76
Verwoerd, Hendrik Frensch 12, 48, 51
Vierdag, G. 10-14, 18
vigilante groups 35-6
Villa-Vicencio, Charles 13, 17
violence 16-17, 61, 71; and churches 42, 61, 71; constructive approaches to 62-5; consumer boycotts 38-9; education 37-8; incidence 31-5; labour relations 39-41; legitimacy of 71-2; political protest 30-41; townships 35-7; *see also* force; non-violence
Vlok, Adriaan 37
Vorster, Dr Koot 51

Watson, V. 24
Webb, Keith 58
Weiland, Herbert 10-14, 18, 81-2
Welsh, David 50, 54-5
Wiehahn, Prof. Nic 40, 99-100, 113-14
Wink, Walter 72, 73-4, 93-4
Winkler, Renate 41, 103
World Council of Churches (WCC) 41-2

Yarrow 91
Young, Andrew 85

Zille, Helen 37-8